PRISON ADMINISTRATION IN INDIA

—Model-Prison Programmes in U.P.

PRISON ADMINISTRATION IN INDIA

MODEL-PRISON PROGRAMMES IN U.P.

DR. B. V. TRIVEDI
Bureau of Police Research & Development
Ministry of Home Affairs
New Delhi

Foreword by
Shri T.N. Chaturvedi
Comptroller and Auditor General of India
New Delhi

UPPAL PUBLISHING HOUSE
NEW DELHI-110002

UPPAL PUBLISHING HOUSE
3, Ansari Road, Daryaganj, New Delhi-110002

The publication was financially supported by the Indian Council of Social Science Research, New Delhi and the responsibility for the facts stated, opinions expressed or conclusions reached is entirely that of the author and that the ICSSR accepts no responsibility for them.

ISBN No. 81-85024-13-8

PRINTED IN INDIA

Published by B. S. Uppal, Uppal Publishing House, New Delhi-2 and Printed at Varshney Printing Press, Vishwas Nagar, Shahdara, Delhi - 32. Composed by S.K. Printing Works, 4/401, Bhola Nath Nagar, Shahdara, Delhi-110032

Dedicated to :

My Father

Vaidya, Shri Ram Shanker Trivedi

&

My Mother

Smt. Kalindri Devi Trivedi

The contents of this book and the opinions expressed therein do not reflect the official views of the Government, the Home, or the police departments. They are the personal views of the author.

Author.

FOREWORD

Prison administration is an essential part of the totality of the criminal justice in any country. It is at the receiving end in a manner of speaking of the police, the prosecution and the judiciary. The processes of prevention, punishment and correction or rehabilitation constitute a continuum. For obvious reasons, and especially since the police and the judiciary represent and command ostensible authority and are always functionally before the public eye, the prison or jail administration unfortunately suffers because of unintended indifference and even neglect. It has taken long for prison administration to acquire a distinctive identity of its own. The significance of prison administration as a necessary and healthy adjunct of crime prevention is being gradually recognised in our social thinking but the requisite back-up it calls for in financial and operational terms lags behind. Prison administration therefore, requires periodical review and reorientation in consonance with emerging social ideals and developing institutional requirements.

The concept of prison administration as institutional device for correction and rehabilitation of the inmates has by and large received only ritualistic homage in the country. In administrative and plan priorities correctional aspects of jail administration have rarely figured prominently. Some how the notion that the jails mainly exist to prevent the culprits and the convicts from doing further mischief has a strong hold on public mind as on governmental working. Occasionally when there is something spectacular like the daredevil escape or jail-break by some notorious smugglers and criminals or dismal episodes of gross ill-treatment of prisoners, abuse of child and women convicts or undertrials, deaths due to callous neglect or maltreatment, riots by convicts etc. that the society wakes up to the nefarious activities in the jails, administrative callousness, nexus of crime and influence, deplorable living conditions, managerial inefficiency, cussedness, etc. It is a pity that the authorities concerned in many parts of the country are hardly able to utilise the paltry funds allocated for repairs and construction of jail buildings, training of staff, initiation of sound reformative measures and the like purposes. I have seen this personally while working as a member of a State Jail Reforms Commission in the sixties or later as Secretary to the Ministry of Home Affairs and Department of Justice, Government of India, in the early eighties. The overcrowding in the jails and the internal working have drawn often exceedingly adverse comments from social workers, the press and the judiciary. But response from the administration for rectificatory action is not always either adequate or appropriate. I do hope that the vigilant public opinion will continually assert so that the recommendations of the Justice Mullah Committee about Prison Administration and Jail Reforms as well as the Financial Allocations by the Eighth Finance Commission to the States in this regard are purposefully utilised. Probably a stage has arrived when the prison administration requires a separate Bureau of its own at the Centre to attend adequately to the problems of research and development of prison administration, modernisation, reform particularly institutionalisation of correctional and rehabilitational approaches throughout the country. It is high time that genuine effort is made to ensure that the status of the prison administration not only meets the present requirements but comes to reflect our social conscience and tomorrow's social vision.

The present work by Dr. B.V. Trivedi is a systematic study of the many issues concerned with prison administration and its modernisation. It provides necessary understanding of the problems and guidance as to how attempt to solve them. The author deserves commendation and congratulations for his useful research in the vital area of jail administration. Modernisation involves development of the capability of the infrastructure and the apparatus and the humanisation and sensitisation of the entire administrative machinery and its approach and attitudes.

Besides providing the historical background and outlining advances in penological thought, it also deals with personnel problems and development, the need for professionalisation, institutional programmes, prison labour, infrastructural facilities within the jails, individualised and reformatory approach to inmates, working out of scientific priorities integral to effective prison administration in relation to ideals of correction, reformation and rehabilitation etc. Though the study is focussed on a particular prison, the author has taken pains to explore the problems of jail administration in all its ramifications and in a wider perspective. Dr. Trivedi has made ample use of the published and unpublished literature on the subject besides extensive surveys and intensive field work. The work under consideration should be helpful in reviewing and streamlining institutional correction endeavour in the country. I do hope this scholarly contribution, informed as it is with practical insights, will be of use and interest to students of criminology, social scientists, administrators and policymakers concerned with prison administration and reforms in a developing country like ours.

New Delhi,
22nd January, 1987.

T.N. CHATURVEDI
Comptroller & Auditor General
of India
New Delhi

ACKNOWLEDGEMENTS

It goes without saying that research undertakings, particularly in Social Science, represent largely a co-operative efforts in which several individuals and organisations contribute. Throughout the course of the present study, I have received help and assistance in such abundance and from so many quarters that it becomes difficult even to mention all the names. I express my gratitude to all of them. I am immensely grateful to Shri B.K. Mishra, the then Inspector General of Prisons, Govt. of U.P., for providing me fieldwork facilities including the availability of official records for the present work.

I am also thankful to Shri B.P. Tewari and Shri S. Prakash, the then Superintendents of the Model Prison, Lucknow and their officers for valuable co-operation in collection of data during field investigation. I am also indebted to the inmate of the Model Prison, Lucknow who supplied valuable information for this study.

I am grateful to the Indian Council of Social Science Research, New Delhi, for awarding me short-term fellowship and an additional grant for computerising of data and supporting publication of the present work.

I offer my humble gratitudes to Prof. M.Z. Khan, Deptt. of Social Work, Jamia Millia Islamia, New Delhi, whose inspiration and valuable guidance have contributed much to the present work. His personal example of dedication and dynamism made working with him an intellectually creative and satisfying experience.

I am deeply thankful to Prof. D.P. Jatar, formerly the Vice Chancellor of University of Saugar for inspiration and for providing necessary facilities to conduct this study. I am obliged to my teachers in the Deptt. of Criminology & Forensic

Science, University of Saugar, particularly Prof. S.C. Tewari and Prof. G.C. Jain for their helpful and encouraging interest in my present work. My thanks are also due to Prof. S. Mallikarjunan for going through the initial draft of the report.

I also wish to record have my deep sense of gratitude to Dr. D.R. Singh, Department of Criminology and Correctional Administration, Tata Institute of Social Sciences, Bombay, and my friends, Dr. N. Prabha Unnithan, Shri V.K. Borwanker, Dr. Bhupendra Gautam and Shri R.D. Shukla who have been a source of unfailing help as well as warm companionship at the various stages of the present work.

I am glad to express my sincerest gratitudes to T.N. Chaturvedi, Comptroller and Auditor General of India, New Delhi, who has been kind enough to accord a foreword to the present work.

I must also express my deep regard for my parents for their unstinting encouragement and emotional substen·nce. I feel obliged in dedicating this work to my parents.

I also grateful to acknowledge the contribution of Shri B.S. Uppal, Uppal Publishing House, New Delhi, for taking personal interest in bringing out the work in print.

Lastly, I also take this opportunity to express my appreciation to my wife Smt. Chandra Kanta Trivedi who exercised examplary patience and understanding, and for being constant source of inspiration and support throughout the progress of the work.

Again, I sincerely owe a debt of gratitude to all of them and many others who remain unnamed.

26th January, 1987 **B.V. TRIVEDI**
New Delhi

LIST OF TABLES

CONTENTS

1

Introduction

In ancient times, convicts used to work the Roman galleys. Till recently working a tread-wheel or crank-box was regarded as exemplary punishment. Early in the nineteenth century, the inmates of the Bavaria camps in the United States of America were deployed on public road construction. So was the case with their counterparts in India. However, work by convicts in both the countries came under criticism for two specific reasons : At the operational level the convicts were required to work under conditions far from satisfactory. Secondly, and most importantly, several administrators, jurists and intellectuals viewed the work by the inmates as causing dissipation of punitive objectives. Nevertheless, in the second half of the last century, work by convicts started gaining acceptance. In contemporary times, in most of the correctional institutions work by the convicts has become almost routine. What, however, differentiates the work by the inmates of modern correctional institutions from that of ancient and medieval times is the approach and the basic philosophy behind the work.

In the ancient and medieval times, when the concept of vengeance dominated penal thinking, corporal punishment, including poetic punishments, used to be the norm. If, however, incarceration had to be awarded, the work and working conditions, invariably used to be dehumanising. Till recently, the theory of deterrence was the mainstay in punishment, including imprisonment. During the period of imprisonment, work was regarded not only as fitting but also essential. Consequently, the form of work assigned to the inmates compared well with the penal objectives : It used to be psychologically dull, often economically unrewarding, and physically exhausting. In the West, towards this, gadgets like tread-wheel and crank-box were devised (see Hibbert, 1963). However, despite the opposition from many quarters for various philosophical and operational reasons, the induction of an economic slant to prison labour could not be helped. Amongst several forms, the prisoners were employed for pulling or pumping of water. Likewise chained gangs of convicts were deployed on public road construction (see Barnes and Teeters, 1966). In India, convicts worked stone handmills to grind cereals.

In the later half of the preceding century, the Elmira movement in the USA marked a watershed in penal thought. It introduced a humane and correctional approach to punishment (for datails, see Korn & McKorkle, 1959). It is important to note that 'work' was the motive force behind the reformatory movement. Earlier, Captain Meconochie had successfully experimented with 'work' in handling the convicts in an Australian penal colony (Mannheim, 1972). Besides, the industrial revolution based on steam-power and division of labour emphasised team-work with little or no room for autonomous work by single individuals and for muted working. From this, the reformatory movement received much impetus. As a result, work by the prisoners came to be regarded as an important means for their reformation. This approach, however, did not go unchallenged. It was argued that the main purpose of imprisonment was 'to supply the prisoner with strong motives for resisting the temptation to break laws'; but because of the reformatory approach, and consequently because of the provision of better food, *employment opportunity* and generally congenial environment, reformatories had turned more into comfortable-havens than penal institutions' (see Haynes, 1935). In due course of time, this kind of opposition however, lost its edge and gainful employment of the inmates became an integral part of institutional correction. Work programmes have, thus, come a long way from some kind of a punitive-repressive slave-labour to become a powerful means to reform and rehabilitate the fallen, and to make them committed to institutions. They signify what Grunhut (1952) terms 'training for work' and 'training by work'.

Nevertheless, vocational training and work programmes continue to attract criticism for being soft or giving concession to the offender, and for being more of a 'diversion' than 'work'. Partly, this betrays the anachronistic notion that offenders are committed to prisons not as punishment, but for punishment, and that to be of penal value, the work in prisons ought to be punitive, exhausting and repressive (Fox, 1952). Moreover, notwithstanding the deprivation of liberty imposed upon the inmates, regulated and directed tasks—light in terms of expenditure of energy—would seldom proffer them the ease and the pleasure which usually goes with leisure-time activities; nor would—or should—the vocational training programmes, if they are scientifically planned and perceptively implemented. The policy statements of the US National Prison Association, the Canadian Correctional Association, the All India Jail Manual Committee and a host of others coming out from forward-looking countries almost unanimously accept 'work' as an important method for re-educating and reintegrating the offenders.

Significance : A modern correctional institution offers a variety of programmes. These include "individual or group therapy sessions, scholastic education, trade or vocational training, maintenance work, recreational and social activities and industrial employment" (official statement of the Canadian Correctional Association, 1965). Keeping in view the psycho-social needs of the inmates, these are designed to achieve the individualisation of the correctional impact. From an abstract angle, they aim to rejuvenate in the inmates the sense of personal worth and dignity. Further, the participation in these programmes instills in the inmates the 'acceptance of norms and values consistent with socially acceptable behaviour' and orients them to 'a life of social responsibility' (Johnson, 1964). Few other institutional programmes would, however, be able to match work programmes in potential, purposiveness and prognosis. "Work in itself", observes Alexander, "is constructive. Productive work means not only physical employment but active occupation of mind as well. Prisoners employed on construction work are better able to avoid the dangers of enforced idleness in custody, they develop and maintain a healthy sense of contribution and usefulness" (1957).

Indeed work programmes concern in the main with the economic aspects of the life of an inmate. In other words, it aims to influence his economic style and capacity, both inside and outside the institution. Nevertheless, the consensus is that it has much to do with his social-psychological makeup as well. (see Khan, 1976).

Work programmes have something to offer to almost every inmate—whether illiterate, literate or educated, unskilled or skilled. Given a large and diverse range, for each inmate there should be available a programme that would best meet his personality needs and rehabilitation requirements. The unskilled would acquire new skills, and the skilled would improve upon what they already have. Even the white-collared would acquire proficiency in some branch of their interest, if nothing else, by way of a useful hobby. There would be many amongst the inmates who are capable but unsystematic, lethargic or downright indolent. The institutional setting through work programmes offers an opportunity to generate in the inmates a capacity for sustained work and to improve their work habits. *Karma* (work) is *dharma* (religion), says the Gita. Work programmes seek to achieve a meaningful reaffirmation of this canon by engendering in the inmates a healthy respect for work. Most of the work programmes are pursued in groups. The group process promotes *esprit de corps* and provides the inmates with inter-stimulation for various group activities (Bogardus, 1949). Through group experience 'rugged individualism' is smoothened into 'socialised individualism' (Bisno, 1952), individual fantasies are brought face to face with social realism (see Brown, 1940), and social antagonism is mitigated to effect a harmonious social adjustment (Page, 1947; Clemmer, 1958).

A work programme, which approximates to the interests of an inmate, makes a deep imprint upon his psyche. It gives him a sense of purpose and a degree of confidence in his own ability to attain and achieve (Jones, 1956). It brings about distinct and positive changes in his "attitude, motivation and self concept" (Switzer, 1967). In sum, it restores his sense of personal worth and dignity.

There cannot be two opinions as to the fact that work programmes have implications which reach outward beyond the individual inmate. The work programmes : (a) facilitate the process of individualisation of the institutional programmes in that an inmate gets healthy and acceptable outlets for his energy and talent, and (b) help in providing an effective treatment to the inmate.

Without being a form of exploitation, or even a conscious means to augment resources (see Tannebaum, 1957), work programmes of their own accord take the institution a step closer to financial self-sufficiency (Heyns, 1964), lessening the burden of the tax-payer (Fox, 1952). Wherever work programmes have been carefully organised, inmates have not only been able to pay for their keep and help their families but also have been able to contribute to the receipts of their institution as its token share in the earnings.

The gain that work programmes contribute to the Gross National Product (GNP) (See Kellerhals, 1959) or that they enlarge alert and constructive citizenry fades in importance when their impact on the process of rehabilitation is considered. They are an indispensable aid to the inmate in overcoming economic, psychological and social obstacles that prevent an effective and meaningful adjustment between him and society. In doing so, they reduce the chances of relapse to criminal ways. They may, thus, represent a major share in the institution's contribution to the overall social response to crime (see also Johnson, 1964). Work programmes, thus, stand out amongst all the institutional programmes. It is hardly surprising to find Sutherland unreservedly enthusiastic in this regard: "If I had to manage prison upon condition that I make my choice of one thing, and only one, as an aid to discipline, as an agency for reform, for its therapeutic value, I would unhesitatingly choose work—just plain, honest-to-goodness work. Of course, I would not like to have to concentrate on a choice, and it would be unwise to be so restricted. Physical examinations, medical treatment, bodily repairs, educational opportunities, spiritual guidance, psychiatry, psychology are necessary and helpful. But the habit of work is what men most need" (1968).

Current Status : In modern times, work in jails is not conceived as additional punishment but as a means for facilitating the resocialisation of the inmates (the first United Nations Congress on the Prevention of Crime and Treatment of Offenders, 1955). It follows that work programmes are in keeping with the modern penal objectives of reformation and rehabilitation. Consequently, in most forward-looking countries, they form an inseparable part of institutional programmes. In Belgium, inmates are required to work to ensure their social readjustment. They are also provided equitable wages, part of which is made available to them for immediate use or remitted to their dependents, and the balance is paid to them on their release from the institution. Finland has a well developed open-institution system for work on public utilities and construction (Soine, 1964). The French Penal Code has been somewhat explicit about work and has changed it into an element of rehabilitation (Talbert, 1973). In Holland, much emphasise is laid on work programmes. Prisoners are offered work opportunities accompanied by suitable wage tariffs to improve their skills and employment potential (Deford, 1962). For juvenile and adult corrections, in East Germany, educational and vocational training is regarded as an important aid for the social reintegration of the prisoners. However, in Italy, work by inmates of correctional institutions is not mandatory. Although it is viewed as an important means of resocialisation, it is offered only to those who are willing to undertake it. In [illegible] inavian countries, work by inmates is an integral part in the institutional policy. The Prison Commission Act of 1958, in Norway, provides for the hiring of inmates by private individuals and concerns. Besides, there are "labour centres" where inmates are put to economically gainful work. In Sweden, the system of Free Work Permit is in vogue : The inmates are released in the morning to work with private employers and return to the institution in the evening. In Yugoslavia, the achievement of work skills is an important criterion in the assessment of the level of resocialisation of the inmates. Previously, mail bag production and repair were about all by way of work programmes in the United Kingdom. However, the correctional system has undergone notable changes in recent decades and quite a large number of 'training prisons' have been organised. These institutions provide training in a wide variety of industrial and agricultural vocations. Reportedly, about 75 per cent of the British inmate population is deployed in productive work (see Jones, 1956).

The USSR has an elaborate correctional labour policy. Comprehensive labour programmes are available for men, women and minors, separately. This apart, there are, mostly in mining areas, special 'labour colonies' to which convicted offenders are sent. Often food rations are measured in terms of the amount of work by them (Koerber, 1934; Deford, 1962).

The work-release programme is relatively popular in Australia. A small proportion of the inmates of jails is released to spend the working day with private employers. So is the case with Canada (Hooper, 1964). But in that country there is also operational a chain of 'work camps' (Baril, 1967).

In the United States of America, work by inmates is almost a routine. There are several systems to put the inmates to useful work. These mainly include lease, contract, piece price, public account, and state use (for details see Task Force Report: Correction, 1967). Within the institutional programmes, federal as well as state prisons evaluate aptitude and personality needs of a fresh entrant after which he is assigned to one of the 72 vocational programmes. A small institution, like the Wallkill Prison, conducts a diversified programme in construction trade, mechanical and repair work, farming, service, and maintenance (Gordon, 1971). There are also functional quite a few 'industrial prisons' (Caird, 1972). As a matter of fact, a concerted attempt is made towards human resource development (Holder, 1978).

The concept of constructive labour has also found application nearer home in Sri Lanka : first offenders with sentences of less than eight months are sent to open work camps where they are given training in agriculture and animal husbandry (*The Indian Express*, 1976).

In India, the inmates are given work in almost all the jails. Ever since, the Indian Jails Committee (1919-20), work has been regarded important in institutional correction. This is what has been reiterated by the All India Jail Manual Committee (1957) and the Working Group on Prisons (1972). As at present, all the inmates undergoing a term of sentence of 'rigorous imprisonment' are legally required to work. In the case of those undergoing 'Simple imprisonment', it is, however, optional. This distinction notwithstanding, the work by the inmates is grouped under three somewhat overlapping categories : (i) inmate service, (ii) maintenance work, and (iii) vocational programmes (Khan, 1976). Short-termers are usually given service and maintenance work, while others (long-termers, lifers, etc.) are assigned to vocational programmes. There are in the country about 1300 correctional institutions, including Central Jails, Model Jails, Women's Jails and Open Jails. Most of these offer vocational training to the inmates. There are traditional trades like blacksmithy, carpentry, weaving and farming; several new trades have also been introduced, including printing, metal casting, tailoring, paper making, tracter repair and animal husbandry.

Generally speaking, an inmate, on entry, is interviewed by a number of custodial and professional staff. Among other things, particulars relating to his previous occupation and vocational preference are recorded. Then a classification committee, ordinarily headed by the Superintendent, assigns him to a work-unit. If assigned to a vocational trade, the inmate starts off usually as an apprentice and gradually moves on to become a 'full worker'. It may be added that there is no class-room instruction or formal examination, and the picking up of skills by an inmate may largely depend on his own motivation.

Bottlenecks: This is not to say that the concept and the practice of work programmes have been accepted without reservations. Often the opinion is expressed that: (i) coercion is implicit in work by the inmates, and (ii) by way of reformation and rehabilitation, they achieve little (See, for example, Orland, 1975). A dispassionate consideration would, however, show that the former argument is totally valid. Law-enforcement, judicial processing as also the fact of imprisonment—all have to have some force or a coercive element so as to be meaningful. Indeed, the issue of what work programmes achieve or do not is a data question. Half a century ago, Gluecks (1930) has found that about two thirds of the men in reformatories, after their release, did not use the trades they were taught; and from the remaining who did use them had been plying them before their entry in the institution. Although reliable data relating to India are not available, the possibility cannot be ruled out that the position obtaining in the country may be equally dismal. However, it would be hasty to evaluate the efficacy of work programmes without going into the snags faced in implementing them. It has been observed that, more often than not, they suffer from several structural and functional bottlenecks (Khan, 1976).

Structure Problems: Insidious and entrenched, problems relating to structure are somewhat basic in character and call for a vigorous reappraisal of the outlook and assumptions underlying work programmes. Doubtless, problems of structure may cause hurdles in the fulfilment of the institutional objectives, adversely affecting the entire gamut of correctional programmes. Most notable among these would be the general attitude of the officials towards the inmates, at all the levels and in all the branches. The idea that criminal behaviour is part of social behaviour is too well settled to necessitate any further reaffirmation. Yet, it is doubtful whether the officials involved in correctional work have managed to get away fully from the medieval misconception which regarded criminal behaviour as the consequence of innate depravity. This being so, it is likely to tell heavily upon the planning and the implementation of work programmes (see also, Kellogg, 1950). In making financial allocations for jails or work programmes, or in supervising the work of an inmate doing a work shift, the attitude of many officials is seen to be far from that of reformative functionaries. This kind of attitude often tends to render the entire exercise futile. Amongst numerous maladies, it may result in 'paper programmes' and 'made work' (see Deford, 1962; Trivedi, 1981). Given this, work programmes may show up on the institutional routine, yet they would qualitatively achieve precious little.

Several characteristics or handicaps of the inmates are offered to explain away any lack of success in work programmes (see Andry, 1963). In India, illiteracy and 'cultural backwardness' are often mentioned (see Pillai, 1959) as major factors impeding the work programme. It seems to be an objective problem. But would it not be, to a great extent, overcome by diversifying the range of work programmes? Also, the malingering by the inmates is frequently brought up. Nonetheless, this problem needs to be examined in relation to the motivational structures of the inmates or, conversely, monetary as well as non-monetary incentives offered to them (see Tappan, 1960; Chapman, 1963). These incentives may well be listed: Monetary incentives usually include regular wages and/or occasional cash reward/bonus (see also, Trivedi, 1977; Unnithan and Khan, 1978). The first U.N. Congress on the Prevention of Crime and the Treatment of Offenders also recommended *equitable* cash remuneration to the inmates (author's emphasis). Non-monetary incentives, although apparently trivial, are greatly stimulating. In the first instance, a carefully selected work programme should by itself be highly motivating. Besides, other non-monetary incentives may be a solicitous gesture, and ego-satisfying word of praise, a proficiency certificate and more tangibly, some remission of sentence. Probably, a balanced 'mix' of monetary and non-monetary incentives would be quite a successful cure for malingering. But do we have a satisfactory system of incentives in correctional institutions ?

Yet another structural problem is that of classification. Based on the study of individual inmates and administered on some well-adjusted system (The National Prison Association, USA), classification is an organised procedure by which diagnosis, treatment, planning and correctional programmes are coordinated and focussed on the individual case (The Manual of Correctional Standards, USA). In other words, a streamlined classification procedure is a precondition for successful treatment of the inmates through correctional programmes. Its concern does not end with the initial diagnosis and assignment. On the contrary, in the light of the inmates' response, it keeps adjusting or even switching the programmes. What is the position in this regard in India ? For diagnosis, do we study the capacity and the aptitude of the inmate, or else, are we guided by the stereotypes like religion, caste, regional affiliation, and so on ? Is the assignment to different work units done in accordance with the needs of the inmates or the manpower demands ?

Functional Problems

Mostly routine in nature, these problems arise during the operationalisation of work programmes. Indeed, such snags may be usual in the functioning of any organisation or scheme. At the very outset, attention may be paid to the range of work programmes made available to the inmates. Reportedly, Soviet Russia has polytechniques exclusively run for the inmates. In the USA there are some four hundred types of vocational programmes. The Wallkill prison in the State of New York, after administering aptitude and achievement tests, initial work assignment and tryouts, offers the inmate a choice for training from amongst 20 different trade courses (see Taft, 1956; NCCD, 1964). In all likelihood, correctional institutions in India would not favour such countries in respect of the range and diversity in work programmes, nevertheless, such a diversity is more than a formal necessity : (a) to meet treatment and training needs (Kellerhals, 1959); (b) to facilitate the rehabilitation of the inmates after release (Fox, 1952); and (c) to synchronise work programmes with the national manpower demands (see U.N., 1955).

Next, a consideration of the inputs that go into work programmes would be relevant. Qualified and experienced manpower is doubtless a critical factor (Nelson, 1966). In many countries, hiring and retention of trained hands in correctional services are reported to be a major problem (see Gels and Cavanagh, 1969). This may not necessarily be true for India in view of the overflowing labour market. Besides, there are quite a large number of industrial and economic state departments, personnel from which can be drawn on a whole-time or part-time basis. The issue of job identification by the staff involved in work programmes, nevertheless, remains a vexing problem.

In recent times, technological developments have revolutionised almost all the modes of economic production, be it agriculture or bee-keeping, soap-making or construction work, or grain-milling or furniture-making. To benefit from technological innovations, we need know-how and facilities. The former is largely taken care of by the trained staff. In the case of the latter, the need for the acquisition or replacement of machines, plants or other gadgets is inevitable. From this stems the problem of capital investment. Has the dispersal of technology been reaching the correctional institutions ?

At present, the market of most of the raw-materials used in various manufactures in India is fairly regulated or controlled. For instance, in Madhya Pradesh, even the jungle-grown teakwood which is valued in furniture-making stands nationalised, and can be procured only from state-owned forest depots. The situation with regard to other raw materials may be even more stringent. All the same, timely, regular and economic supply of raw-materials to correctional institutions running work programmes is vital. Few correctional institutions in the country complain about this, perhaps supply of raw-materials has been smooth or, alternatively, indifference towards work programmes has been cushioning its impact.

In the USA, two major stumbling blocks have been often reported in the outflow of the goods and services from the correctional institutions : (1) slender market demand for the goods (Glaser, 1964; Heyns, 1964) chiefly due to considerations of quality and price, and (2) resistence by the labour organisations to inmate-services being floated in the open market (Hibbert, 1963). Condition in India, however, are a shade different. The trade union movement in the country is yet not stong enough, but, notwithstanding the fact that at present India is a sellors' market, the former point merits consideration. Rarely have the goods produced at the correctional institutions been reported to be stock-piling. Nonetheless, a few sales peculiarities may well be kept in view. Bulk-orders from the government departments or undertakings shield these goods from open market competition. Despite under-pricing, backed up by government subsidies, only a small portion of these goods finds an indifferent sales-opening through a chain of state-run 'jail industries' emporia. Moreover, 'production in most of the institutions has few norms; as such, production capacity' varies with the size of the order book, and henee, there is no visible idle capacity.

Of late, several marketing management techniques have been envolved. These include building up a sales network, undertaking regional/local level, advertising, organising a sales promotion campaign, making market assessments and the like, to generate a sizable and steady demand and to sustain and step up the production. Have these techniques found their way into the management of jail industries ? In the USA, a government-supported but autonomous undertaking, the Federal Industries Incorporated is reported to be operating profitably (See Deford, 1962; Wenk and Frenk, 1973). In the State of Uttar Pradesh in India, similarly, a Jail Development Corporation has been established. Perhaps this kind of facility calls for further expansion and streamlining.

Lastly, a brief reference may be made to the administrative policy governing correctional institutions and thereby work programmes. To organise work and to help the inmates to help themselves, is a substantive task (see Tappan, 1960) which underscores the need for a goal-oriented policy. As India has predominantly the state account system for the utilisation of 'inmate-power, the government has special responsibility to keep the policy relating to work programmes as purposive and in tune with the new demands coming up in the wake of political, technological, economic and social changes. By definition, policy is a frame work for action (see Freeman and Sherwood, 1970; Ranney, 1968). A perspective policy is, therefore, necessary for tackling present problems in a given organisation since it is able to anticipate problems in the long run. Most of the problems mentioned earlier would be found to be partly or wholly linked with the policy issues. Has the state-policy relating to work programmes been clear, balanced efficacious ?

LITERATURE SURVEY

Over the years, a considerable body of literature has grown, which deals with institutional correction including their evolution, organisation and working. Even in relation to prison labour or work programmes, a large amount of data has been accumulated. For example Mc Clean (1964) provides a detailed account of the origin, rationale and mode of training for certain categories of convicted offenders. Theoretical considerations underlying work by the inmates of jails have been highlighted by many writers (see, for examples, Goffman, 1961; Sutherland, 1968; Sykes, 1978). Tabasz (1975) has attempted a mathematical model to evaluate the economics of prisons and prison programmes, including work programmes. The policy issues concerning work programmes as a production sub-system have been delineated by Duffee (1975), Miller, (1972) and many others.

Significance of vocational training programmes and work for the resocialisation of the inmates in correctional institutions has been reiterated by many including Sutherland, (1968); Deimling, (1973); Wellford, (1973); Wofe, (1978); and Carney (1980). That work in institutions is a means to achieve 'vicarious expiation' has been underlined by Else and Stephenson (1974). Konopka (1974) regards correctional programmes, including vocational training, as important measures to reclaim the social 'casts off'.

The reformative and rehabilitative value of work programmes has been emphasised by several writers and researchers (see, for example McCollum, 1973, Glaser, 1977). A few studies also show that the inmates are equally aware of the significance of work programmes (among others, see Bernhardt, 1969).

A large number of accounts are available describing the mode and modalities concerning work programmes in practice in different institutions and countries. Some of them have been referred to earlier. These apart, a few focussed studies are also available. The importance of incentives in work by inmates has been underlined by many writers (McGrath, 1965; Brando, 1967; Singer, 1977). Wenk and Frank (1973) have collected empirical evidence which brings out that cash incentives are not only a definite aid in stepping up inmates' participation in work but are also instrumental in changing certain behaviours in the desired direction.

It may be pointed out that quite a few studies are available which bring up evidence to the contrary, that is, vocational instruction and work achieve little or nothing by way of reformation and rehabilitation of the inmates (Bold, 1952; Morris and Hawkins, 1970; Orland, 1975).

In the Indian context, many researchers have focussed attention on prisons. More or less following the model postulated by Clemmer (1958), many studies have been attempted (Shrivastava, 1971; Shrivastava, 1977; and Singh, 1979). Focussing attention mainly on the state of Maharashtra, Datir, (1978) provides a comprehensive account of the prison system. More specifically, work programmes, as organised in the Central Prison, Madras, have also been studied (Khan and Unnithan, 1978, Unnithan and Khan, 1979).

It is obvious that work programmes in jails as a means of reformation and rehabilitation have not received the amount of research attention they deserve. Aspects like the range of the available trades and their relevance, the method of assignment of inmates to different trades, their involvement in work, the impact of the former on the latter, and the like have seldom been studied in depth. This inadequacy appears to be more so acute in the context of such a large jail system as in India.

PRESENT WORK

The preceding account has outlined the importance of work programmes to institutional correction. The potential of work programmes to reform and rehabilitate inmates in enormous, yet they have not been fully exploited. Also, scientific literature available on work programmes particularly in India, is far from being comprehensive. Motivated by these considerations, it is proposed to study work programmes in the Indian social context with following main objectives :

(a) to gain familiarity with the Model Jail as a community;

(b) to look into the personal characteristics of the inmates;

(c) to study the custodial as well as treatment staff and their orientation to correctional objectives;

(d) to identify institutional goals and the strategies governing work programmes as a means to fulfill correctional objectives; and

(e) to examine the impact of work programmes on the inmates.

It may be restated that prisons often tend to be a community or society in themselves. This is reinforced by the emergence and continuance of informal organisations and cliques, differentiated norms and practices, and the like. Yet another feature which stands out in the Indian context is the system of 'convict officers'. Inmates are appointed convict-watchman, convict-overseer, or convict-warder. Apart from status, they also enjoy certain privileges. The practice has somehow managed to survive the severe criticism which has been levelled against it eversince the Indian Jail Committee (1919-20). Besides, the critical influence of the system can hardly be ignored in a study of prison as a sub-cultural phenomenon. It would be recalled that work by prisoners has been a routine for centuries. However, what differentiates work as a means of reformation from servile work as a punitive measure is the approach. Whatever the approach, it would be reflected in the budgetary allocations, personnel policy and prison routine. Like-wise, personnel aspects may be enquired into. The Weberian model of bureaucracy has been in vogue for long. With the changes in social conditions, the inadequacy of the model has become apparent in several areas. This is particularly true for welfare organisations including these engaged in correction. That correctional functionaries need to discard the bureaucratic style and attitudes, and adopt a welfare approach has often been emphasized. The welfare approach which the correctional functionaries have been able to imbibe, would be reflected in their role norms, their job identification and their perception of a successful correctional career.

Further, to organise work programmes in jails on economically productive lines (see Tappan, 1960) is a substantive task, which calls for a goal-oriented policy, and to operationalise it, for the adaptation of interrelated development techniques like planning, programming, implementation and evaluation (for details, see Ranney, 1968). The process of planning and programming, in order to be effective needs to take into consideration (i) the techno-economic feasibility within the institution, and the relevance of the programmes to the conditions obtaining outside the institution (see also, Kellerhals, 1959; Barnes and Teeters, 1966); (ii) the resource—position, finance, material supply and trained manpower (Nelson, 1966); and (iii) the human material, namely the inmates. Towards a speedy and efficient implementation of programmes, a part from trained manpower, timely and adequate supply of material and streamlined marketing facility, what is needed most is the involvement of the inmates. In turn, the inmates' motivation appears to hinge upon a number of factors, such as their physical fitness, aptitude (this underscores the process of classification), available monetary and nonmonetary incentives (see Chapman, 1963). Besides, systematic and periodical evaluation of a programme in terms of its cost-effectiveness serves as an indispensable feedback which provides a basis for decision for its continuation, modification or expansion (Freeman and Sherwood, 1970). A judicious use of these development techniques is likely to enable work programmes to yield rich dividends. Also, these form a substantive concern of the present study.

In the light of the experience gained through the pilot study, the present work proceeds on the following main hypotheses :

(1) The institution offers conditions conducive to the furtherance of correctional objectives.

(2) The inmates have the background and capacity for the work programmes available in the institution.

(3) The custodial as well as vocational staff are sufficiently oriented in the reformatory ideals.

(4) In their organisation and working, the work programmes in the institution are purposive and inmate-oriented.

(5) The positive impact of the work programmes on the inmates is determined more by the offence and work-related factors than by personal factors.

It may be added that originally, jails in India were organised primarily on the deterrence model. Following the report of the Indian Jail Committee (1919-20), correctional ideas were superimposed on the existing organisation and structure. Of late, much emphasis has been laid on reformation and rehabilitation. However, it remains to be seen whether the jails in the country are able to translate into practice what they progress. In the reformation and rehabilitation of the inmates, correctional programmes are indeed important. What is, however, of even greater importance is the approach with which jails are organised and how these function. This calls for the point of view of the jail-staff as well as that of the inmates. These may be ascertained and supplemented with observational data so as to secure an insight into conditions conducive to correctional work.

Work by the inmates may represent with equal ease either a mode of servitude or a means of reformation. Of course, the vocational staff may be there to impart instruction or to direct the inmates to participate in work programmes. Germane to the issue is, however, the approach with which they go about to discharge their duties. At the same time, the point may not be lost sight of that vocational staff do not make for all the officials who interact with the inmates. In fact, their proportion in the total staff strength may be small or very small. Thus, while a study of the predisposition of the vocational staff is important, equally important is the study of the predisposition of the custodial staff.

A reference has already been made to the limitations imposed by the lack of aptitude, capabilities and interest on the part of the inmates. Certain scholars are even categorically of the opinion that the inmates are downright malingerers. This needs to be looked into a little more closely. Nonetheless, the inmates' response to work programmes may well not be analysed in isolation—the work programmes themselves need to be appraised for their adequacy. If the programmes match the background and the personality-needs of the inmates and if they are inmate-oriented, they would at their own evoke much interest among the inmates. It is from this angle that they need to be enquired into.

A dependable estimate of the effectiveness of work programmes is likely to be had through a post-release study of the inmates. Nevertheless, this being beyond the scope of the present study, attention needs to be paid to the changes the work programmes have been able to make upon the opinion of the inmates about work programmes, their capacity to equip them better for readjustment after their release, and the like. By collecting information on these dimensions, it should be possible to secure data relevant to the hypotheses listed earlier.

Coverage : The present study focuses on the Model Prison, Lucknow, in Uttar Pradesh. It may be noted that Uttar Pradesh is one of the pioneering states in the country as far as the reformation of convicts is concerned. The state has initiated many progressive schemes in the field of the treatment of offenders and the prevention of crime. On the other hand, crimes reported to the police are maximum in this state (see *Crime in India*, 1977). Further, the city of Lucknow has a long history of affluence and culture. This background of the Model Prison may well be kept in view. As the name itself suggests, the model Prison has been organised, with considerable forthought, to reform the offenders. It has a set of rules. Firstly, only those offenders who commit heinous offence are housed. These offenders are selected from various prisons in the state on the basis of their conduct in these institutions. It follows that the institution does not house under-trials. Secondly, the living conditions are changed from maximum security to minimum security as the behaviour of an offender shows improvement. Thirdly, a range of educational and vocational facilities are provided to the inmates. Fourthly, the long period of stay of the inmates in the Model Prison enhances the impact of the correctional programmes. Fifthly, the willing convicts, who send petition to the authorities for their transfer into the prison, are accorded permission only after initial screening.

All the inmates and staff members of the Model Prison have been included in the sample: 337 inmates and 120 staff members. Main characteristics of the inmates are : most of them (86.3%) have been convicted for the offence of murder; and almost every one of them (99.4%) is a first offender. Noticeably, 75% of them have been involved in group offences. Given this, many of them (86.6%), naturally, are lifers.

Due to long terms of sentence, the inmate-population is relatively stable, a fact which may help inmates to undergo long-term treatment programmes. Besides, in the institution there is qualified and trained staff to look after the inmates. These are some of the considerations which have gone into the selection of the institution for the present study (see also, Chapter III).

Data collection: For collection of primary data for the study, the mainstay has been the technique of structured interviewing. As such, two interview schedules, one for the jail staff and the other for the inmates, have been drafted. The schedule for the staff has covered such dimensions as demographic and personal aspects (independent variables) and the perception of the staff in respect of their professional success, their interaction with the inmates, the place of the convict officers and the significance of work programmes (dependent variables). On the other hand, the schedule for the inmates has covered the demographic aspects of the inmates, particularly relating to their offence and their work assignment (independent variables) and on subcultural aspects of the jail, their perception of the role of the staff, inmates and convict officers, and their views of different correctional programmes including work programmes (dependent variables). After pretesting, editing and standardisation the schedules have been rendered in Hindi. Besides, schemata for doing observation and preparing case records have been worked out : the former is meant to bring out different jail routines and the latter, to trace the progress of new entrants through various institutional routines.

Collection of secondary data was synchronised with the familiarisation trips to the institution during which a deliberate attempt was made to identify informal groups, cliques and leaders in the jail population.

Analysis : The data was marshalled and edited to remove inconsistencies. The analysis of the secondary data was done through classification, tabulation, and some amount of computation. However, for analysis of the primary data, based on single classification principle, a code book was developed. This incorporated mostly simple variables and a few composite variables. For the latter, the cutting points and the mechanics were specified.

The interview data for the study emerged from two samples: jail staff (N=120) and inmates (N=337). While editing interview schedules, the endeavour was to maintain the respondents' view, Wherever responses have been ambiguous or irreconcilable, these have been treated as invalid or inapplicable.

Using the SPSS (H) Programme (See Nie et al., 1970), the data were processed at the Council for Social Development, New Delhi (total computer time, about 2.17 hours). In the first instance, mono-dimensional tables or marginals were taken. After going over the distribution of the variables, the tabulation plan prepared earlier was readjusted wherever needed. In the light of the objectives and the hypotheses, the data processing mainly involved preparation of two and three-dimensional tables and statistical calculations of measures like proportions, measures of central tendency, bivariate differences, correlation, etc.

The general procedure adopted during analysis was to examine the relationship of each major variable with three variable-configurations : personal, offence-related and work-related. While interpreting variables of examining linkages between variables, bibliographic and secondary materials, wherever relevant, were drawn upon.

Since the computer output of cross-table was too enormous for the limited space, only the variable-distribution was given, and the presentation of two and three-dimensional tables was deferred, although statistics derived from them, wherever relevant, were utilised. Further, relationship between two or more variables was focalised only when the probability of null hypothesis proving true was 10 per cent or less and when the association (contingency coefficient) was 0.10 or better.

The study has seven sections including Introduction (Chapter I) and Conclusion (Chapter VII). To what extent the Model Prison represents a distinctive group phenomenon has been highlighted in Chapter II. To be a means of behaviour modification and to be an aid in the reassimilation of the inmates in their post-release period, work programmes have them, the inmates as the main referent. Also, the extent to which work programmes are effective would depend on the background and the capacity of the inmates. This has been examined in Chapter III. Chapter IV focuses on the jail staff. It may be reiterated that both custodial and treatment staff exert influence on the thinking and conduct of the inmates. Their background, motivation and commitment to the correctional role may make all the difference as far as the outcome of the institutional programmes, including work programmes is concerned. Next, attention has been paid (Chapter V) to the work programmes and support facilities available in the institution. In spite of quite a few theoretical and logistic limitations, Chapter VI attempts to provide an assessment of the impact of work programmes on the inmates. In doing so, the thrust has been on delineating the nature and extent of change in the conduct of the inmates, as assessed by them and the staff. The references cited in the text are listed at the end of the report.

2

The Model Prison

The jail system in Western countries is commonly traced to the Poor Houses in England during the regime of Queen Elizabeth I. They housed not only the offenders but also paupers. The inmates were provided food and clothing and were also required to work. Within a short period of their existence, these institutions, however, greatly deteriorated and were severely criticised for their sub-human conditions. Eventually, separate institutions were organised for undertrials and convicts. The officials of the East India Company brought the system to the subcontinent (Khan and Chilad, 1982). In the Second half of the eighteenth century, they established jails in the regions of Calcutta and Madras. In 1836, the East India Company constituted a Jail Inquiry Committee to look into the system and to suggest ways to streamline it. However, the recommendations of the committee could not be fully implemented because, among other things, the company rule was, in 1858, replaced by the Crown Rule. The later half of the nineteenth century was marked by a number of fact-finding committees. To be specific, in 1864, 1877, 1888 and 1892, enquiry committees/commissions deliberated on the jail system. At this stage, it would be relevant to recall that during this period the Elmira Reformatory was established (1878) and reformatory ideas were gradually gaining acceptance not only in the USA but almost in the entire Western world. As a consequence of the aforementioned enquiry committees or perhaps due to the Elmirah movement, the maiden legislation the Prisons Act of 1894 was brought on the statute book. Another noteworthy piece of legislation is the Prisoners Act of 1900. Nonetheless, it is doubtful that reformatory ideas were able to influence the system sufficiently, till 1919. The Indian Jail Committee (1919-1920) was a landmark in jail development in the country. The committee forcefully advocated for a correctional approach in jails. Following its recommendations the subject of jails was transferred from Central Government to State governments, the constitutional position which has continued ever since. In the post-Independence period many states appointed their own fact finding Committees/Commissions. The Central government, by way of its advisory role, also constituted the All India Jail Manual Committee and a Working Group on Prisons and organised several conferences.

About 1,300 jails for the reformation and rehabilitation of the offenders who are committed to them, are functioning in the country. These provide a variety of correctional programmes to the inmates, including quarantine and classification, educational programmes, vocational training, religious education, self government and the like. In order to motivate the inmates to change their thought and behaviour, jails also provide such incentives as remission, temporary release, privileges and wages of sorts. Since it is important to see whether jails are able to realise the reformatory objectives, the present study proposes to discuss it in relation to the Model Jail, Lucknow. In order to keep the discussion focused, it may be hypothesised : *The institution offers conditions conducive to furtherance of correctional objectives.*

Before proceeding further, the dimensions relevant for the examination of this hypothesis may be outlined. That prisons are a part of the criminal justice system which is a part of the government and which in turn is a part of the society, is a mere reiteration of a well known fact. What is, however, not so well known is the fact that a prison often tends to become a society in itself. Being a part of the criminal justice system, a prison has a formal organisation and specified functions to perform. In it often several undercurrents are discerned. The inmate population may have informal organisations including cliques. It may have its own norms, values and practices. From these may flow distinctive relationship patterns, conduct norms, parallel economy, and inter-personal conflicts and harmony. These are the dimensions which were focalised nearly four decades ago. Donald Clemmer viewed the prison as a community and delineated the life and organisation of the inmates in a prison (1958). Likewise, Gresham Sykes has paid attention to maximum security prison and has outlined its distinctive features as a society of the captives (1958). In the Indian social context, attempts have been made to study prisons with almost similar premises (Srivastava, 1977; Singh, 1979). Of late, much emphasis has been laid on studying a prison as a 'total institution' (Goffman, 1961). These and similar studies bring home the fact that apart from formal objectives, organisation and functions, prisons may have something much more beneath the surface. The informal organisation and conduct norms may have a direct bearing on the realisation of the correctional objectives. Argued differently, the success of correctional programmes, including work programmes, would greatly hinge not only on the administrative policy and support but also on the informal social milieu, making for a sub-culture of sorts in a prison. Apparently, the latter aspect has not attracted sufficient administrative and research attention. In any case, in reforming and rehabilitating offenders, prisons have met almost everywhere with indifferent success. In recent times, their ability to change and reintegrate offenders has been seriously questioned. As a matter of fact, a movement termed deinstitutionalisation has been gripping penal thought and practice. These are some of the dimensions which have been explored in relation to the Model Prison, Lucknow.

FORMAL ORGANISATION

In India, there are sub-jails (mainly meant for undertrials),

District Jail Class II, District Jail Class I (housing under-trials as well as convicts, mainly short-termers), Central Jails and Special Jails including Model Jails (mainly for long termers and lifers).

The Institution under study, a Model Prison, is in the State of Uttar Pradesh. The State is the largest in the country in terms of population (110,858,019) which is one-sixth of the country's population (683,810,051). The literate population is also large, that is, 30,358,013 (Male—22,845,887, Female—7,512,126) and the total rate of literacy is 27.38% (Male—38.87%; Female—14.42%). It may be noted that the better part of the state, and more specifically, district Lucknow, housing the capital of the State, had been under the Muslim rulers in the medieval period and under the British administration for more than a century and half. Few other population characteristics are that the State is predominantly rural in character (Urban=19,973,223; Rural=90,912,651) and has a large segment of scheduled caste population. The State has a high literacy rate but is usually regarded as economically backward. In 1977, 2,22,621 cognizable offences were reported which work out to be 224.8 offences per 100,000 population as against the national average of 202.5. Perhaps, these population characteristics may reflect in the inmate population. The role of Uttar Pradesh, the heartland of India, during the different periods and ages of its long history, has been dynamic. It has contributed extensively to Indian culture in the past and is now humming with activities for economic, social and cultural development.

It is difficult to assert that the state has been forwardlooking in regard to correctional programmes. Although it has subjails (3), district jails (50), Central jails (5), Open camps (2), Model Jail (1), Bal Sudhar Vidyalaya (1), Juvenile Institution (1), Jail Training School (1), and Nari Bandi Graha (1) which is associated with the Model jail at Lucknow, it has been somewhat lagging in the overall development of correctional programmes. Though the U.P. Children Act, 1952 has been adopted, yet sufficient juvenile services have not been provided. Likewise, probation services are also somewhat indifferent. The provision of one juvenile institution and one Bal Sudhar Vidyalaya is hardly satisfactory in view of the size of the state. It would, therefore, be hardly surprising to find that juveniles and young adult offenders are often housed in jails along with adult offenders.

Lucknow, situated on right bank of Gomti, has a population of 10,06,843 (Male=5,48,891; Female=4,57,952) with rate of literacy of 57.14 (Male=64.03; Female=48.89) both of which are lower than its nearby industrial metropolis Kanpur. However, sex ratio of Lucknow is higher than Kanpur and population density (per Km^2) is also higher than Kanpur, Gorakhpur and other nearby districts (798) (Census, 1981).

Setting : In dealing with work programmes some importance has to be given to the physical setting which forms part of the work-climate (Anastasi, 1964). Lucknow's Model Prison is one of the peculiar institution not only in Uttar Pradesh but also in India, which is running on some specific correctional premises. In 1949, this institution was set up in the old central prison building with a new correctional programme.

The Model Prison is located at the outer part of the Lucknow city on Jail Road, in between the Charbagh Railway Station and Alambagh. At a distance of about 2 or 3 Kms from the Model Prison, one District Jail and one Jail Training School are situated. The Jail is divided into four parts, known as *Bhawans* i.e., Reception', Jamuna', and 'Ganga' inside the walls, and another section called 'Bihari' Bhawan, outside the walls. But as the reception building is old and in dilapidated condition, this section has been merged with the 'Jamuna Bhawan'. Gradations and functions of each parts are as follows :

(A) *Jamuna Bhawan* : When the inmates come from another jail either on transfer or conviction, firstly they are kept in this section. This section is a maximum security section. There is maximum watch and ward and only custodial staff looks after the inmates.

(B) *Ganga Bhawan* : This section is less secure. There is no provision for convict officials (CW, CO, CNW). The inmates are promoted on the basis of good conduct and behaviour and sent from 'Jamuna Bhawan' to this section. They are called 'Adarshi Kaidi'. They are allowed to move freely and to work in trades inside the section.

(C) *Bihari Bhawan* : This is the minimum security section. There is no watch and ward or custodial staff to look after the 'Bihari Kaidi' or inmates. Because they are considered reformed, they can move freely and are allowed to live in barracks outside the jail walls. They may find their work outside the jail, even in the city. The main work assignment of these inmates is agriculture, and they daily work on the farm.

As would be seen a little later, this is a big jail which covers a total area of 157 acres. Of this, the main prison and ancillary buildings take up 40 acres and 10 acres, respectively. Beside this, open field area of nearly 67 acres is used for agricultural purposes and about 30-40 acres of land is adjoining the jail walls. Of course, it is a walled institution : it has an outer wall which is about 18 feet high and also an inner wall. It would be seen that the institution had been holding an inmate population almost equal to its capacity. For example, on July 1979 the actual inmate population was 355 while the authorised accommodation of the jail is 343 (see Table 2.1). This is mainly due to the lack of remand, undertrial and short-termers. As a matter of fact, there is no problem of over-crowding in this institution as is seen in many other jails. The jail has the facility of a telephone. Most of the jail building is electrified.

Accommodation

Water supply in the jail is through the tube-wells. Previously the inmates used to pull the water themselves. Now the wells are fitted with electric pump. Tap-water is supplied by the tube-well which is supplemented by the overhead tanks for storing drinking water. Although, there are 8 wells, out of which 6 tube-wells are under construction within an area of 500

TABLE 2.01

Showing authorised accommodation available at the Model Prison, Lucknow.

Name of Ward	Authorised Accommodation	Actual populaion
Jamuna Bhawan	100	100
Ganga Bhawan	200	200
Bihari Bhawan	25	25
Hospital	18	30
Total	343	355

Source : Office of the Superintendent, Model Prison, Lucknow.

metres. Their depth is also said to be conversing with each other, with the result there is little likelihood of any of them working normally, resulting thereby a loss of some Rs. 3 lakhs to the national exchequer, as reported by the jail officials. In spite of these arrangements, water supply is a problem, particularly, during the summer season. All inmate blocks have flush latrines (20) supplemented by one set of urinals in each circle. These facilities are looked after by the inmates themselves. At present, only two flush latrines are in working condition. Some time ago, flush latrines have been provided in each circle but these proved a failure due to scarcity of water, caused mainly by the casual electric supply and widespread ruptures in the old and dilapidated pipeline. Also, due to inadequate height, the gas outlet pipes on the sanitary pits greatly pollute the air.

Personnel : Treatment staff is there to initiate programmes directed at reformation of the inmates; nevertheless, custodial and administrative staff are equally important. Treatment staff, custodial staff and administrative staff together make for the general milieu of the institution which would impart a correctional influence upon the inmates. Let us have a look at the organisational structure of the Model Prison, Lucknow. The Superintendent is at the apex of institutional organisation (see Diagram I). Subject to laws, the Uttar Pradesh Jail Manual and the overall direction of the Inspector General of Prisons, U.P., the Superintendent takes decisions in all matters concerning control and supervision of the staff, upkeep of inmates, their discipline, jail expenditure, etc. In the discharge of his duties, he is assisted by a Deputy Superintendent who shoulders some of his responsibilities. The next executive officers are the jailors (2) to whom some of the duties, including posting of warders, distribution of inmate labour, inventory of raw materials and production, custody and maintenance of fire-arms and ammunitions, jail purchases, maintenance of jail records etc., have been delegated. In turn, they are assisted by Deputy Jailors (5). To look after various custodial and administrative functions, such as office, store, watch and ward, there are eight Assistant Jailors. Lowest among the custodial staff are warders. They include one Chief Head Warder, One Chief Head Warder (Arms) and 18 other Head Warders. The Chief Head Warder posts Warders, and apprentice Warders, assists the Jailor in unlocking, counting, locking up of inmates as well as distribution and recording of labour and duties among the prisoners. The Chief Head Warder (Arms) looks after the security of the prison, fire-arms, etc. By way of fire-arms, the jail armoury has 44 muskets (.410 calibre). The gate-keeper maintains the gate-register, mentioned earlier. 90 Head Warders and Warders (Grade I-18, Grade II-56, Grade III-16) carry out the actual watch and ward work. The jail office, formally speaking, has only a Office-Superintendent and an Accountant. The jail hospital has Medical Superintendent (1), Assistant Medical Officers (2), Compounders (2), and Staff Nurses (2). The jail school has higher grade teacher (1), and secondary grade (5), Instructors (9), including a Mission teacher who deals with the Raj-Kaman, Lorry-driver and Lorry-Assistant who are in the rank of a warder. There is no other professional staff like Welfare Officer, Social Worker and Psychologist in this institution.

The jail has 9 Convict Night Watchmen, 28 Convict

DIAGRAM I

Showing the organisation of the custodial staff in the Model Prison, Lucknow

Superintendent

|

Deputy Superintendent

|

Jailor————————Jailor

|

Dy. Jailor—Dy. Jailor—Dy. Jailor—Dy. Jailor—Dy. Jailor

|

Asstt. Jailor—Asstt. Jailor—Asstt. Jailor—Asstt. Jailor—Asstt. Jailor—Asstt. Jailor—Asstt. Jailor—Asstt. Jailor

|

Chief Head Warder————Chief Head Warder

|

————18 Head Warders————

|

————56 Warders————

|

————16 Apprentice Warders————

Overseers and 6 Convict Warders. Appointed on the basis of conduct and behaviour, these convict officers assist the jail authorities in many ways. Conspicuous for their Red cap and Yellow '*Kurta*', they are seen every-where—at the gate of the office, hospital, stores and factory sheds. Convict Officers enjoy certain privileges, including additional remission in their term of imprisonment.

Budget : For budgetary purposes the expenses incurred on jail industry are indicated separately. A perusal of Table 2.02 would show that 'extra expenses' is a major budget head and the expenses on the upkeep of the inmates (including Rs. 1.75 per head per day on food according to a specified scale, see U.P. Prison Manual) are met from this budget head. This apart, attention may be turned to the overall expenditure pattern of the institution. If we ignore the increases in the staff allowances, additional expenditure due to 'MISA Bandis' and purchases of raw material, the jail budget appears to have remained almost unchanged over the five year period under discussion.

Proceduras : The prison process involves a large number of interrelated sub-processes. The adequacy or otherwise of a given sub-process is likely to affect other sub-processes as well. On the other hand, taken together, these sub-processes make for the correctional milieu in the institution and for the success of the prison process. A description of these sub-processes is likely to give an insight into the institutional functioning as well as it would enable us to look into the work programmes in a proper perspective.

(a) *Admission* : After an offender has been sentenced to imprisonment or transferred from some other jails, he is

TABLE 2.02

Showing details of the budget of the Model Prison, Lucknow for the financial year 1978-79

Year	Budget Heads	Amount in Rupees
1978-79	1. Tools and Plant	6,000=00
	2. Contract Contingency	26,800=00
	3. Raw Material	9,20,000=00
	4. Wages	2,10,000=00
	5. Tools	71,000=00
	6. Factory Miscellaneous	1,49,000=00
	7. Maintenance of Vehicle	10,000=00
	8. Extra Expenses (Dietary+Hospital+Clothing and Bedding+Sanitation+Miscellaneous charge+Moving prisoners).	6,50,000=00
	Grand Total	22,42,800=00

Source : Office of the Superintendent, Model Prison, Lucknow.

brought to the jail by the police. The Deputy Superintendent and the Jailor verify the particulars in the court order or transfer order and give a receipt to the police. The particulars of the offender, including his personal description and marks of identification, are entered into the admission register. He is required to change into the prisoner's uniform. His own clothing and other personal belongings are listed, sealed and deposited with the jail office for safe custody. Next, the jail medical officer examines the inmate and records, in the admission register, the state of his health and any physical or mental abnormalities observed. According to the U.P. Prison Manual, the medical officer also indicates whether the inmate is fit or unfit for work. Following this, the inmate is provided with a history ticket and assigned to a cell-block or barrack. He is also issued bedding and utensils. The admission register is countersigned by the jailor and approved by the Deputy Superintendent of Jail every day.

(b) *Classification* : After admission formalities are completed, the inmate is interviewed by the Jailor and Dy. Superintendent and they decide on the basis of report as well as recommendations of the Medical Officer as to what work the inmate may be assigned to, according to their educational background, skills, experience and job-preference. Classification of the inmates is made on the basis of their good conduct and their past behaviour as recorded on their history tickets (in case of those inmates who were on transfer from the other jails) in the institution.

(c) *Correctional Services* : In contemporary times, jails aim at the objective that the persons who come in conflict with law should be afforded an opportunity to change themselves so that they are eventually reintegrated into society. With this end in view, apart from food, clothing and shelter, the jail under study, offers a variety of correctional programmes. Education level of the inmates is often cited as a pre-requisite to successful learning of work. A portion of a barrack is earmarked for the jail school, housing also the jail library (4,278 books in Urdu, Hindi and English languages), newspapers and magazines (see Table 2.03). The present institution has a recognised school for adults staffed by six teachers. It is equipped to teach illiterates and literates. Instruction programmes follow usual adult education methods. The easier letters or the alphabets are taught first followed by the more complicated ones. The inmate is taught to write his own name in the beginning. They are divided according to their literacy level. The medium of instruction is Hindi. There is a course of primary education of three months' duration for literate inmates in this institution. The inmates, after passing this course, can get teaching assignments in other jails. But for illiterate inmates, there is a training course of four months' duration. After completion of this training period, they are eligible to appear in the examination, conducted by "Adarsh Praudh (Adult) Training College", Model Prison, Lucknow. The inmates, who get through in this examination, are awarded a certificate under the signature of the Inspector General of Prisons and Superintendent of Prison. According to the teachers of the institution, these literate trained certificate holders carry on the teaching in the inmate blocks in the evening and they are getting remuneration amount of Rs. 2=00 per month for their teaching assignments. The school also acts as a reading room and library. The jail school provides facilities to the inmates to learn drawing and painting, monoact play, and physical training. That general education has attracted the attention of the inmates is reflected in Table 2.04. This angle has been pursued during the interviews with inmates (See Table 2.05). Only 6% of them report that they

TABLE 2.03

Showing details regarding books in the library at the Model Prison, Lucknow for the year 1978-79

	1978	1979
Number at the beginning of year	4,301	4,283
Purchase	Nil	Nil
Disposals/Condemned	18	05
Number remaining at the end of the period	4,283	4,278

Source : Office of the Jail School, Model Prison, Luckuow

TABLE 2.04

Showing the number of inmates who studied in the prison school during the last 10 years (from 1970-1979).

Year	Illiterates	Literates	Total
1970	36	25	61
1971	24	15	39
1972	16	13	29
1973	21	15	36
1974	09	10	19
1975	05	08	13
1976	06	02	08
1977	09	08	17
1978	07	05	12
1979	06	06	12
Total	139	107	246

Source : Office of the Jail School, Model Prison, Lucknow.

are attending the jail school. Obviously, it indicates the low priority the jail administration attaches to this programme.

It hardly needs mention that all are not apparently well with the educational services in the institution. A part of the school building is not suited for teaching purposes, because there is not enough space for library, reading-room and class-rooms. This has resulted in the curtailment of facilities. It was also noticed that teachers do not take interest in the teaching of inmates seriously and often confine themselves to mere distribution of magazines and newspapers.

While Sutherland (1968) is enthusiastic about work programmes he also considers that "Physical examinations, medical

TABLE 2.05

Response of the inmates to the question, "Do you attend the school here ?"

	No	Yes	Total
Frequency	317	20	337
Percentage	94	06	100

treatments, bodily repairs...are necessary and helpful." With this in view, medical and health services available in the institution may be discussed. The prison hospital has 28 beds (authorised accommodation, 18) for indoor patients. It would be seen from the Table 2.06, the daily average population from September, 1978 to April, 1979 is somewhat downward or decreasing but overcrowded for indoor patients. According to medical officers, most of the medical problems treated include gastritis, fever, asthma and veneral diseases. The serious cases are sent to the General Government Hospital, Lucknow, which is nearby, with a Warder or police escort. The problem of malingering by inmates is recurring and calls for special caution on the part of the medical staff. As reported by medical staff, they are able to cope with the number of patients they get every day and are well stocked with drugs and medicines. They are provided with 4 literate inmates and 2 compounders, who act as orderlies. The duties of the medical staff, other than treatment, include looking after the general hygiene of the institution and its sanitation, certifying inmates for their fitness to work, checking the institutions' diet, recommending extra or special diets for prisoners who medically requires it, and assisting the classification board.

Since diet is often considered part of the health services, we shall take a closer look at it. The menu of this institution consists of :

Morning Meal : 3 days in a week Daliya, Gur and 4 days gram.

Afternoon Meal : Dal, Chapaties, Rice and one Vegetable.

Evening Meal : Dal, Chapaties, Rice and one Vegetable.

TABLE 2.06

Showing the daily average attendance of patients in the prison hospital

Year and Month	Outdoor	Indoor	Daily average
September, 1978	1554	53	53.63
October, 1978	285	37	10.38
November, 1978	921	48	32.30
December, 1978	1045	90	36.61
January, 1979	941	33	31.42
February, 1979	695	12	25.5
March, 1979	756	28	25.0
April, 1979	861	11	29.0

Source : Office of the Hospital, Model Prison, Lucknow.

Accordingly, every inmate gets cereals as mentioned below :

700 Grams Wheat flour, 90 Gms Dal with Chapaties or 120 Gms Dal with Rice, 470 Gms Rice, 60 Gms. Daliya, 45 Gms Gram, 30 Gms. Gur, 240 Gms. Vegetables, 14 Gms. Salt, 1 Gm. each Haldi and Chili, 7 Gms. Oil and 3.15 Gms. Coke per day. In 1978-79, the feeding cost of an inmate was Rs. 1.75 per day.

Let us now take an overview of the programmes available in the present institution. Work programmes in the jail may be described under three broad groups :

(1) *Inmate service* : On an average day 40-45 inmates may engage in the community kitchen, godown/store and in clerical jobs, while 36 in laundry, mulahiza, hair-cutting, including

convict overseers, convict warder and convict night watchmen services, totalling 82.

(2) *Maintenance Unit* : Sixtythree inmates are detailed for sweeping, cleaning and sanitory work in different barracks and in the jail as a whole.

(3) *Vocational trades* : A large number of inmates (192) engage in different types of industries available in the institution e.g., spinning and gauze bandage (33), oil-press machine (15), powerloom dyeing (37), weaving (35), paper making (13), tailoring (16), baan kaman (4) and agriculture (39).

The jail also offers religious facilities. During festivals, the inmates may be provided with special food. For the Muslim inmates a *Maulvi* visits the jail on the *Idd* days to lead the prayer. Likewise, on the Christmas day a *Padre* comes. Besides, there is no full-time preacher to deliver lectures on moral issues, i.e. the lectures are only delivered either on festivals or some special occasion. There is no temple inside the jail.

By way of recreation, "a well rounded programme in any prison...must include a carefully thought out recreational programme..." (Barnes and Teeters, 1966). The present institution offers both indoor and outdoor facilities e.g., Volley-ball, Kabbadi, Chess, and Carrom. There is an open-air theatre and is used for film shows and cultural activities initiated by the inmates themselves, including plays and skits. Inmates are allowed to listen to radio programmes and to see T.V. programmes on every Sunday and Thursday. The inmates also have a music party, i.e. Orchestra or Band who also give programmes outside the jail even in the city. However, these facilities do not appear to have generated much interest or involvement among the inmates as would be seen from Table 2.07. Notwithstanding the facilities provided by the jail, the inmates have their own ways of spending their leisure time. Some of them, for example, may join together for a session of devotional songs, others may play *Kabaddi* and the like.

The inmates also have a self-government. There exists what

TABLE 2.07

Response of the inmates to the question, "Do you take part in any of the games/sports/other recreational programmes in this jail ?"

	No	Yes	Total
Frequency	278	59	337
Percentage	82.5	17.5	100

is known as the Inmate *Panchayat* (the assembly). Inmate self-government or the system of 'Inmates' *Panchayat*' is the visible expression of the prisoners' self-determination and co-operation in all matters concerned with life in the institution (Vidya Bhushan, 1970). The Panchayat system is said to be very advanced in Uttar Pradesh Jails; especially in this institution, Panchayat system is working well. It consists of four 'Panchas' headed by one 'Surpunch', totalling 5. They are not elected, they are nominated by the Superintendent of Jail. Regarding nomination of Panchas, it is learnt that there is no fixed time schedule and date. It is made, whenever, any Panchayat Office-bearer has been charged for any misconduct or is released from the institution. It is, however, not clear what is the role of the Panchayat or its place in the jail administration.

Jail permits inmates to meet relatives and friends. In the Jail parlance, it is known as 'interview'. The jail, however, does not have a visitor's room. The inmates are ushered into an office room where they stand by a grilled window and their visitors on the otherside. Under instruction of the Deputy Jailor, the 'interviews' are usually supervised by the Convict Officers. Officially, the inmates are not supposed to accept any food, money or gifts from their visitors.

Remission (good days) is conceived as a positive incentive "for good behaviour and work" (GOI, 1957). Nevertheless, it is a concession granted by the government and is subject to forfeiture. Remission is given to all inmates at the rate of 6 days a month, 3 days for good conduct and 3 days for industry and performance. In the case of convict officers, the remission is allowed at the following rates: (a) Convict Warders—10 days a month; (b) Convict Overseers—8 days a month, and (c) Convict Night Watchmen—7 days a month. Inmates engaged in service, working as cooks, sweepers and the like, and those who work on Sundays and holidays, receive 7 days per month additional remission. A prisoner, who has committed no offence in the prison or has continuous good conduct, receives 15 days a year as additional remission. This apart, there are provisions for special remission as well. The Superintendent of the Jail may allow a special remission of up to 30 days in a year or the I.G. Prisons upto 60 days to a prisoner who assists in the maintenance of jail discipline, in running jail industry, in preventing fire and the like. In relation to special remission, several innovations have also been introduced. For example, the inmates who undergo sterilisation operation are allowed an extra remission of 15 days. The record of all types of remission received by the inmates is maintained by the Octagon Officer (Chakkar Officer) of the section who adjusts the date of release accordingly.

Towards discipline, appropriate custodial and organisational methods are adopted. This aside, the inmates are also awarded several forms of punishment. In the present case, most of the inmates have been punished for possessing money or contrabands, for quarrelling among themselves, for negligence in work, particularly in work shifts, for assault and, applicable for only to convict officers, sleeping while on duty.

Routine: The jail routine begins with the morning alarm which rings around 4.45 A.M. Soon the barracks are unlocked at 6.00 A.M. and then a headcount is taken by the warders. When the inmates are through with their morning ablutions, the morning meal is served around 6.30 A.M. Meals are distributed by the inmates themselves. The inmates then form themselves into gangs in accordance with the work assigned to them and reach their work places at 7.00 A M. Their number and turnout is recorded in a labour register by the Chief Head

Warder. The morning work session usually begins at 7.00 A.M. and may continue till noon. On return to their barracks for their mid-day meals, they may relax for a while before the second work session begins at 1.00 P.M. to 5.00 P.M. They are again counted and returned to their blocks. They are allowed to have a bath or a wash before the evening meal at around 5.30 P.M. They have some leisure till 6.30 P.M. when they are yet again counted and locked up for the night. In each block, there are convict night watchmen who take turn to see that nothing untoward happens during the night hours. Besides, outside the locked doors of the inmate blocks, warders keep vigil.

On Sundays and holidays, inmates are free to spend their time the way they like. They may play games, listen to the radio in the reading room or watch TV (only on Sundays and Thursdays).

Although the Superintendent of the Jail daily inspects the jail but also on certain days of the week he inspects the parade of the inmates. Theoretically, they may bring to his notice any complaint they might wish to and it is his duty to verify and possibly redress it. In practice the situation may be, however, a little different.

Subculture : That jails are an identifiable social microcosm with certain distinctive features (Murton, 1976), that each of them sustain their own isolated social structure (Wellford, 1973), and that there prevails an unwritten inmates code around which life in jail moves (Holt, 1977) has been often focalised. Keeping in view the position that inmates in many jails may have evolved a system of their own for conferring status, a code governing interpersonal relationship and standards of behaviour, it would not take long to adduce the existence of a distinctive normative structure. Gunther and Gunther (1974) report clandestine activities in penal institutions. These may often result in the sudden outbreaks of disturbances (Zeeman et.al., 1977). At times they may make for some kind or 'counter-society' (Harding le Riche, 1975). That there exists in jails an underground economy has been reported by a large number of researchers (see for example, Sykes, 1958; Holt, 1977; Gleason,

1978). Besides, the process of prisonisation is reported to have as much a demoralising effect on the inmates as well as on the staff (Haney, et.al., 1973). It is demeaning and dehumanising for all concerned (Schmidt, 1971). Farmer (1977) reports that correctional work engenders some sort of cymicism among the workers; and Shellack and Berry, mention "Spiritual Castration" (1972). For the inmates the problem may be a little more acute. They may have poor self-esteem and low morale (Macht and Seidl, 1977). The 'pain of imprisonment' may bring about among the inmates a pervasive sense of alienation (Korn and McCorckle, 1959; Hymn, 1977; Carrol, et.al., 1979). To what extent these theoretical positions or field conditions obtain in the Model Prison of Lucknow, may be examined.

Informal Structures : After the Superintendent, the position of the Deputy Superintendent is seen as most important. Responsible for the management within the jail, for the maintenance of the inmates and for the assignment of duties to the custodial staff, he is doubtless important in jail administration. This apart, the entire custodial staff is found to be preoccupied with security. Often it may overshadow the reformatory function of the jail or even the maintenance of records in the office. It follows that the treatment staff occupy only a second place. As a matter of fact, a kind of antagonism between the custodial and treatment staff characterise the relationship between the two. Also, the treatment staff rarely fails to point out that most of the administrative work is shouldered by the convict officers (43). So is often the opinion of many of the inmates. On the other hand, convict officers represent an interesting institutional practice. It has survived the incessant criticism eversince the Indian Jails Committee (1919-1920). The U.P. Jail Manual lays down that 10% of the inmates may be appointed as convict night watchmen, overseer or warder on the basis of their conduct. Since the appointment carries certain privileges, every inmate aspires for it. Furthermore, different levels of custodial functionaries take active interest in this—often their views and recommendations as to who should be appointed Convict Officers are not similar. This may even lead to a mild intrastaff conflict.

By way of treatment staff, there are in the jail only two functionaries : vocational instructors and teachers. The vocational instructor is a lower-rung functionary, who reportedly is more interested in the output than in imparting of instructions to the inmates. The teacher, also a lower-rung functionary, has much to say about his field of activities. He feels that educational programmes in the jail is mainly optional. He himself is drafted for office work and sundry chores.

The Superintendent inspects the weekly parade of the inmates. So is done by the D.I.G. and the I.G. Prisons when they happen to visit. During these parades, the inmates are allowed to come out with the problems they have.

Attention may now be turned to jail routines. In the name of classification, there is little to be mentioned. Attempt has been made to follow new entrants into the jail through successive stages over a period of 40 days. Apart from the assignment to a barrack or the *Bhawan* many new entrants are not talked to by custodial and treatment staff for days together. They themselves are found at a loss as to what they are supposed to do.

The jail has limited but somewhat advanced correctional services. The vocational instructors, it may be restated, appear to be more interested in the work completed than skills taught. Side by side, general education of the inmates enjoys only a second priority. In sharp contrast, prison discipline is given much emphasis. Apart from formal means to discipline the inmates which have been referred to earlier, there are informal means as well. Several instances have been reported when nonconforming inmates have been knocked about by the warders and convict officers.

Norms and Values : The inmates have quite a few norms of behaviour which are somewhat unique. The majority of the inmates are Hindus and therefore caste conscious. Few inmates would be prepared to take food prepared by the members of the lower caste inmates, particularly Sudras. This aside, they also differentiate each other in terms of their being undertrials or convicts. The two categories of inmates often find each other at a distance. Almost a similar differentiation is found to exist between different categories of offenders. For example, those who have been convicted for murder, dacoity or other heinous offences are held with some kind of awe and respect.

Almost all the inmates nurse a sense of injury against society irrespective of the fact whether or not they have actually committed the offence they have been convicted for. They hardly need a prodding to come out that they have been given a raw deal, that they have been made a scapegoat or that they have been penalised which many others in similar circumstances are able to make away. Most of them have much to say against the police and judiciary but not as much against jail officials.

Amongst themselves, few inmates are reticent about their doings and undoings. A given inmate, for example, may narrate to other inmates the criminal occurrence without inhibition. The life in prison characterised by a fellow feeling is sustained by the relative adversity of the circumstances. More often than not many share gifts they might have received from visitors or nurse an ailing fellow inmate. Strangely enough, quite a few inmates tend to become highly religious.

Patterns of relationship: A brief reference to the comaraderie among the inmates has been made earlier. This should not lead to the inference that jail community is wholly free from human failings. Often undertrials are seen trying to order about the convicts and, on the other hand, some convicts when provoked gang-up and give good thrashing to some undertrials. Also, quite a few inmates try to extract money, particularly from the newcomers. Interestingly, there are quite a few inmates who offer such services as that of charperson, washerman, masseur and the like-against cash or kind.

Spying by the inmates for the jail officials is a phenomenon which has attracted much research attention. Perhaps, there are situational compulsions both for the officials and the inmates. The former seek information in order to stall or curb unwanted activities, and the former are drawn into the grapevine so as to secure favours and privileges. Apart from the actual existence or the efficiency of such a grapevine, inmates often entertain mutual suspicion on this account. This is what is borne out by the data presented in Table 2.08. It

TABLE 2.08

Response of the inmates to the question, "Do you feel that there are inmates who pass on information about other inmates to jail authorities ?

	Most of them	Some of them	None of them	Total	NR
Frequency	10	189	134	337	04
Percentage	3.0	56.8	40.2	100	(1.2)

would be seen that 56.8% of the inmates feel that there are some inmates who have been acting as 'stool pigeons'. This fact may have some repercussions on the interpersonal relations of the inmates.

Convict Officers : Apparently Convict Officers (COs) are there mainly with the idea that they would serve as a bridge between the officials and inmates and that they would be more understanding and friendly with the inmates and also in practice the situation is somewhat same. Table 2.09 brings out interesting details. A majority (86%) of the inmates feel that the Convict Officers behave with them as brother, friends or social worker. On the other hand, some 14 2% of them report that they deal with them as officers, master and boss. This may also be supported with the opinion of the officials : a vast majority of the jail officials feel that Convict Officers behave with the inmates as brother, friend, or social worker. It reflects the positive influence on inter-personal relations of the inmates as far as the Convict Officers are concerned. This may also support the healthy correctional practice in the institution under study.

Convict Officers have a role almost in every area of the jail administration. They guard the main gate, attend to officers,

TABLE 2.09

Response to the question, "In your opinion Convict Overseers/Convict Night Watchmen/Convict Warders behave with others as......?"

Source	Responses (Percentages)						Total	NA
	Stranger	Brother	Master/ Boss	Friendly	Social worker	Officer		
Inmates (N=337)	—	52.3	2.8	33.1	0.4	11.4	100	(16.6)
Officials (N=120)	—	67.5	0.8	27.5	4.2	—	100	(—)

oversee work in sheds, supervise food distribution, distribute medicine and fruits in hospital, decide on the disposal of the produce from the kitchen, garden and so forth. It would be readily seen that they have much scope for being helpful or troublesome to other inmates, or for being instrumental in exploitation and in corrupt practices. Yet another important function shouldered by the Convict Officers is to help the inmates to meet and talk to visitors (commonly termed *mulakat* or interview). The scenario as it obtains in the present institution may well be kept in view. By the main jail office, there are a few duly barred windows which are used for this purpose: the inmates face their visitors standing on the outside and talk to them. The latter are not supposed to receive any gifts of cash or kind. Usually the whole process is supervised by a warder with the help of Convict Officers who accompany individual inmates from their barrack/workshed to the interview-window. Are they actually helpful in this ? The data presented in Table 2.10 bring out a divided opinion. A majority of inmates (56.8%) and 90.0% of the Officials think otherwise. The reasons are obvious : in spite of jail rules, gifts are passed on by the visitors to the inmates and Convict Officers, more frequently than not, ask for and exact a cut.

The C.O.-inmate relationship is more or less characterised by

TABLE 2.10

Response to the question, "Do you think that the Convict Night Watchmen/Convict Overseers/Convict Warders are helpful in arranging interview ?"

Source	Responses (Percentage)		Total	N.A.
	Yes	No		
Inmates (N=337)	43.2	56.8	100	2.4
Officials (N=120)	10.0	90.0	100	—

disagreement or even conflict. It may be a matter relating to general behaviour, discipline or work, or the distribution of food, medicine and fruit or cut in gifts, there would be occasions when Convict Officers and inmates would not see eye to eye with (especially in Jamuna Bhavan). The observational data repeatedly indicate the existence of such conflict situations. This has also been ascertained through interviews. (See Table 2.11). It would be seen from the data that 82.7% of the inmates feel that Convict Officers do not get displeased with them, and on the other hand a sizeable number but very few (16.4%) of them admit that Convict Officers often get displeased

TABLE 2.11

Response to the question, "Do Convict Overseers/ Convict Night Watchmen/Convict Warders get displeased with other inmates ?"

Sources	Responses (Percentage)		Total	Can't say	N.A.
	No	Yes			
Inmates (N=337)	82.7	16.4	100	0.9	2.4
Officials (N=120)	93.3	6.7	100	—	—

with them. This has been further ascertained on the part of jail officials of the institution. Jail officials (93.3%) also report that Convict Officers do not get displeased with the inmates. It indicates that there is a healthy mutual adjustment between them.

Inmate-Staff relationship : Both custodial and treatment officials are there to help inmates to change. On the other hand, there are certain inherent contradictions underlying this relationship. Generally speaking, custodial staff is constantly suspicious of the inmates and the treatment officials regard them as perpetual malingerers. Nevertheless, the two have to interact. The officials were asked as to how much of their duty time they spend in contact or conversation with inmates (see Table 2.12). More than one-fourth of them report that none

TABLE 2.12

Response of the officials to the item, "How much of your duty time is spent in contact or conversation with the inmates ?"

	None	Not much	Half of it	Most of it	Total
Frequency	05	27	11	77	120
Percentage	4.12	22.5	9.2	64.2	100

or not much of their time is devoted to this; and about 64.2% of them state that most of their working time is spent on this. This may not be taken to be a very satisfactory state of affairs. Towards exercising a therapeutic influence, contact or conversation is just a starting point. This aside, have the officials been helping the inmates to improve their conduct and behaviour ? Table 2.13 represents the opinion of the inmates in this regard. It is found that 56.1% of the inmates feel that most of them do so. What is more notable is the fact that in the opinion of 22% of the inmates none of the officials move in this direction. This hardly suggests that inmate-staff relationship is optimally being made use of in reforming the inmates.

TABLE 2.13

Response of the inmates to the question, "Do you think officials help and guide inmates to improve their conduct and ideas ?"

	None of them	Some of them	Most of them	Total
Frequency	74	74	189	337
Percentage	22.0	22.0	56.1	100

This is not to say that inmate-staff relationship is always ambivalent or inimical. Among the inmates there are many who become favourites of the officials. In this, prime movers occasionally are conduct and behaviour and frequently certain other considerations. Among these extraneous considerations, the background of the inmates, their main offencc, body-build, general behaviour, links with the outside community and the capacity to grease the palm of the officials are some of them. It may be noted that it is the combination of these characteristics which matters taken singly, many of them would become counterproductive. To a good deal, these observational data match with the interview data. Nearly more than one third of inmates (see Table 2.14) report that there are among them inmates who are favourite to jail officials. This kind of attitude of the officials towards the inmates being determined by the considerations other than their conduct and behaviour would often tend

TABLE 2.14

Response of the inmates to the question, "Do you think that amongst the inmates there are some who are favourite to jail authorities and some are not ?"

	No	Can't say	Yes	Total
Frequency	197	25	115	337
Percentage	58.5	7.4	34.1	100

to become a partisan attitude or partiality. This may manifest while disbursing benefits, privileges, appointment to the position of Convict Officer, assignment of job/trade and so forth. The opinion of the inmates has been ascertained whether the officials (usually custodial staff) show partiality in the assignment of job/trade to the inmates (see Table 2.15). While more than three-fourths of the inmates do not report partiality in such matters, 11.6% of them do indicate the presence of it. In a matter like this, even a minority opinion of the present magnitude may well not be ignored. Is this kind of partial attitude also extends to work programmes ? Table 2.16 brings out the opinion of the inmates with regard to the distribution of work by the instructors. Indeed, majority of the inmates deny that the instructors adopt a partial attitude in such matter. Only 2.7% of inmate think that he adopts partiality. Both the assignment of job/trade and the distribution of the work in sheds,

TABLE 2.15

Response of the inmates to the question, "Do you find that the authorities show partiality in the assignment of job/trade to inmates?"

	Yes	Can't say	No	Total
Frequency	39	11	287	337
Percentage	11.6	3.3	85.2	100

TABLE 2.16

Response of the inmates to the question, "Do you find that training officers show partiality in the distribution of work ?

	No	Can't say	Yes	Total
Frequency	293	35	09	337
Percentage	86.9	10.4	2.7	100

become suspect for partiality and favourtism because, among other things, there is operational no proper system of classification. On the whole the nature of inmate-staff relationship in the jail appears to have much scope as it is for improvement.

Corrupt practices in correctional institutions particularly in jails are not wholly unheard of. As such, the institution under study may also not be altogether free from this malady. The observational data indicate areas where there is scope for shady practices; further they are usually suggestive and only in a few cases specific. Nonetheless, they do bring out practices which are important to a systematic understanding of jail subculture.

Many inmates report that the inmates are not given full ration (Wheat-flour, rice, cooking oil, sugar etc.) as officially shown. Usually what happens is that, due to underweighment or under-issue, the ration meets the requirement beyond the specified period; for which periodically a fresh indent is placed with the contractor-supplier; who prepares an invoice accordingly; which is entered into the registers at the jail gate and at the store without supplies being actually received; and the ration or its cash value being distributed among the rank and file. The jail hospital has also not been wholly free from malpractices. Reportedly, medicines (particularly vitamines tablets and tonics), fruits and milk have found their way to officials. The jail also has a sprawling vegetable garden. The produce is meant for the inmates as well as for the officials who are supposed to pay for them but at a concessional rate. However, the possibility can not be ruled out that officials get vegetables gratis. So might be the case with such services like that of blacksmith, carpenter, washerman and so forth. In quite a few cases inmates have been reportedly working as orderlies or even cooks at the residence of officials.

Inside the jail, after the Superintendent, Deputy Superintendent and Jailor, the most important functionary is the Octagon Officer (Deputy Jailor in rank). All the Deputy Jailors vie with each other for this posting. It is prized because among other things the Octagon Officer is responsible for computing remission of the convicts, and his opinion/recommendation in the appointment of Convict Officers matters. On either count he can make lot of money were he is so inclined.

Similarly, there would not be many inmates who would give a clean chit to jail hospital and the medical officer. The medical officer has the authority to prescribe to the inmates rest. Outside the jail he may be approached by the relatives or friends of a given inmate or may be approached through a Convict officer on hospital duty. Reportedly, both the doctor and the Convict officers are able to make good money. In any case, many a stout inmate is seen exempted from work or on hospital diet.

Whatever the extent of shady practices in the jail and whatever the shady areas, the Convict Officers have a key role. In a few cases, it has been observed that these Convict Officers encourage officials to start or accelerate corrupt practices. The reasons for this are not far to seek : they stand to gain equally. This apart, the COs on 'interview' duty have sometimes a finger on the pie.

Practices : One of the popular passtime of the inmates is, indeed, chatting together. Among other things, this makes for an efficient channel of communication. The inmates are equally animated about the remission and the date of release of each other. They may discuss as to who has been given and how much remission and why. Many inmates are found to be not-so-optimistic about their post-release prospects. They may speculate about the attitude of the family members, the community, the police and the like. Nonetheless, the most popular subjects are found to be jail officials and Convict Officers. The accounts of their doings, undoings and misdoings tend to travel fast and reach to the inmates sooner or later.

It goes without saying that the inmates are seldom satisfied with the quantity or quality of the food they are provided. They may like to have a full rice dish or a special diet on festive occasions-both may not be always forthcoming. Similarly, there may be a smart inmate who may attempt to receive food a second time. Most inmates feel that during 'emergency'

(1975-77) both quality and quantity of food had improved.

In any case, the 'food story' concerning the Convict Officers is entirely different. Some of the Convict Officers reportedly maintain their own store/kitchen. They may arrange milk from the hospital and tea leaves from outside-often with the help of jail warders themselves. Not only tea but also full meals may be prepared separately by and for the Convict Officers. During the course of data collection, the investigator was severally entertained by the Convict Officers to fruits, tea and the like.

Underground economy in correctional institutions has often been reported. Gleason (1978) has provided accounts about the hustlings in a Michigan prison. According to Holt (1977) not only does a parallel economy flourish in prisons but also among inmates there are enterpreneurs, merchants, peddlers, loan-sharks and the like. Almost all the inmates have money with them in varying amounts. The long-termers and the Convict Officers reportedly keep with them large sums of money. Obviously, this contravenes jail regulations. As such, when officials are overtly active and personal search is frequent, the inmates look for hiding places: The most preferred ones are the linings of the clothes and the underside of the wooden badge which every inmate bears on his chest.

The inmates need money for a number of things. These may include : chewing pan, tobacco, cigarettes, soap, hair-oil or even addictive drugs. They may need to pay to the inmates in the jail kitchen so as to get better food. Still others may need money to bring round a passive homosexual. There are, in the main, two ways by which money reaches the hands of inmates. Relatives and friends may pass on cash during 'interview'. Secondly, the relatives and friends of inmates on instruction may personally give money or even send money-orders to jail warders. Interestingly, the Convict Officers have a role in this as well. Many of them reportedly do not need any assistance from their relatives and friends; on the contrary, quite a few of them are reported as making remittances to their family.

In spite of jail regulations, various forms of intoxicants do manage to percolate into the jail. A new comer in the beginning may face difficulty in maintaining his habit but as soon as he is able to get into the prison life, these difficulties may not remain acute. This aside, many inmates are addicted to alcohol and cannabis. Usually, they are able to get the drug of their choice in a number of ways. Some inmates are able to circumvent the security during 'interview', and receive their supplies. Yet another supply source, reportedly, is the jail warders themselves. This apart, small quantities of drugs change hands against cash, kind or favours.

The inmates may usually be forced to take to homosexual activities. Lifers and toughies, who are often Convict Officers as well, may play 'tiger' and the effiminate or youngish inmates may play 'punks'. In this the working of the police is also responsible, at least indirectly: usually dealing rural, tribal and illiterate people the police records their age as 18 years or above, so as to avoid proceedings under the Children Act. Consequently, many young boys, get processed and imprisoned with adult offenders who in many cases use them for their pervert activities. Tigers often adopt a plausible strategy. They may see to it that the targeted inmate gets lesser food and facilities and harder work. After a day or two they may step in with a benevolent posture offering better food, drugs or even money. At times, direct action like beating and assault may also be resorted to.

Life in the jail has brighter moments as well. Occasionally the state publicity department may screen a feature film or a well meaning citizen may visit them to give a song recital. Many inmates celebrate festivals like Janmasthmi, Raksha Bandhan with gusto. In their own barracks they may place and decorate huge pictures of gods and goddesses, take much pains in organising a 'havan' or Chipin small sums of money to have elaborate *Prasad*. Similarly, national festivals like Independence Day and Republic Day are celebrated with great zeal (these also carry added motivation of additional remission). For days together, they may rehearse small skits and dramas to be staged on the festival day. The female roles in such performances have also to be played by the inmates. Most touching, for example, however, is the occasion of '*Raksha Bandan*'. The inmates are visited by their sisters or the female inmates of the '*Nari Bandi Grah*' who tie *rakhi* on their wrists and give them sweets.

The foregoing account dealing with formal and informal aspects of the institution under study may well be kept in view while looking into work programmes as a therapeutic device. Physical setting, personnel, procedures, services and the like, combine to have a direct bearing on the institutional milieu. Equally important in this are the sub-cultural aspects. Less visible but all pervasive, informal structures, norms and values, relationship patterns, clandestine going on are the sub-cultural elements which have a decisive influence on the motivational structure of the inmates and, therefore, on the nature and extent of their involvement in various institutional programmes. Taken together, the foregoing analyses hardly encourage the conclusion that the jail under study offers conditions which would truly facilitate the realisation of correctional objectives. The hypothesis under examination is not supported. Never the less, the profite of the institution presented here may provide a meaningful backdrop to our understanding of the institutional dynamics and programmes.

3

The Inmate

For discussing work-programmes in a correctional institution, a delineation of the antecedents of the inmates is more than a formal necessity. Pillai (1959) has studied prison labour in South-East Asian Countries including India. While describing extramural activities in Indian Jails, Saksena (1960) has also discussed work. Likewise, the studies of Shrivastava (1971), Srivastava (1977) and Singh (1979) dwelt upon work programmes in passing. There are available a few official reports as well. Besides, a few empirical studies have also been conducted. Nair (1969) has studied the role of prison industries in the rehabilitation of discharged prisoners. Some data on work programmes and inmate capabilities in the central prison, Madras, are also available (Khan and Unnithan, 1978). It would be noticed that not much of empirical and focused data are available relating to the correctional institutions in India. Much less scientific information is to hand regarding the inmates' role, their capability and their interest in work programmes.

This section focuses on the inmates of the Model Prison, Lucknow. Mainly descriptive, it sets out to examine the following hypothesis : *The inmates have the background and the capacity for work programmes available in the institution.* It is assumed that personal characteristics, family background and the role-perception of an inmate precondition the level and quality of his participation in the work assigned to him in the institution. This is what is proposed to be examined in the light of the data collected in the present study.

Personal Characteristics : An inmate in such an institution usually finds himself in a peculiar situation. He is almost totally insulated from the mainstream of the community life. His world shrinks to within the four walls of the institution. His routine is governed, on one hand, by the rules and regulations of the institution and, on the other, his conduct and behaviour are influenced by the norms and values that permeate the inmate group. Needless to add that the former is formal and the latter is informal. Indeed, the response to these two concurrent forces would vary from inmate to inmate. It follows that personal characteristics of the inmates are important, for several reasons and switching from normal community life to prison life may be traumatic. To get into the institutional routine may not always be non-problematic. Often the near-regimentation in most institutions stands in sharp contrast to the life in community outside. As such this may make heavy demands on an inmate. Again, the amenability of the inmate to prison routine would be determined by his psycho-social background. Lastly, personal characteristics of the inmates are particularly important when the issue of correctional impact is considered. He would be able to benefit from different correctional programmes and would be able to change his thinking, behaviour and life style as facilitated by his background. This becomes pointedly relevant in the context of the acquisition of work habits and skills. It would, therefore, be fitting to analyse a few important personal characteristics of the inmates in the jail under study.

Age : Aday (1977) finds age important in a little more specific way : He reports that younger inmates are almost weighed down with numerous problems of adjustment in the institution, and the older inmates are found to be overly concerned with the problems they are likely to face when they return to the community on release. Besides, younger inmates, more often than not, may have more hostile feelings towards society, legal system and even the institutions. They may frequently indulge in assaultive behaviour (Mabli, 1979). This may, on one hand, cause adjustment problem and, on the other, raise difficulties in the individualisation of the correctional impact. These angles may be examined in the present context.

A perusal of Table 3.01 would show that the inmate population in the jail is largely oldish, more than half of them is above 30 years in age, while 44.2% of them is below 30 years of age. This trend is further supported by the average (28 years). This is both problematic and promising. The young jail-population (44.2%) may be more vociferous. On the other hand, since most of the inmates are not old, they are likely to be more amenable to change and, therefore, receptive to correctional programmes.

TABLE 3.01

Age of the inmates (in years)

	15-20	21-25	26-30	31-35	36+	Total
Frequency	03	65	81	64	124	337
Percentage	0.9	19.3	24.0	19.0	36.8	100.0

It would be of more than a passing interest to examine whether the age of the inmates is linked with other factors. It is seen that age and education are highly significant but inversely related (tau= —0.67626; $p<0.0180$) in that the level of education among the young inmates is higher than the older ones.

Attention may now be turned to shady aspects of human behaviour. The use of intoxicants does not appear to have any linkage with the age of inmates while the marital status of them is significantly associated with the age of the inmates (tau= —0.16309, $p<.0001$). It would be seen that the inmates, who are in middle and upper age groups, are usually married. The age of the inmates shows good deal of relationship with the offence committed by them (tau= —0.08831; $p<.0076$). This is to say that both old and young inmates are found to be involved in heinous offences like robbery, dacoity and murder. This, however, is not linked with the term served as the latter has shown little variation with age.

Lastly, the present work assignment of the inmates may be examined in relation to their age. Although this has good deal of association with their age (tau=0.08218; $p<0.0164$), no clear trend exists to suggest that inmates in a given age group are assigned a particular job. Apparently, the correctional institution, while assigning inmates to different work programmes, is not guided by consideration of age of the inmates.

Religion : Religion is important to human beings, including inmates of jail. According to Tylor, it is the belief in superior beings (1930). To Fraze, religion is the propitiation or reconciliation of powers superior to man which are believed to direct or control the course of nature and of human life (1950). Of greater relevance to the present context is the concept provided by Malinowski; "Religion", he writes, "is a mode of action as well as a system of beliefs, and a sociological phenomenon as well as a personal experience" (1926). Further, quite a few religions are seen to have a capacity to reconcile certain forms of anti-social behaviour and religious tenets. In other words, an individual may be religious or even highly religious and may concurrently also persist in certain form of crime.

It is seen from Table 3.02 that 80.4% of the inmates are

TABLE 3.02

Religion of the inmates

	Christian	Hindu	Muslims	Sikh	Others	Total
Frequency	02	271	61	03	—	337
Percentage	0.6	80.4	18.1	0.9	—	100.0

Hindus. This proportion is far more than the proportion of Hindus in the country population (82%). Conversely, other religious communities including Christian, Muslims and Sikhs are, so to say, under-represented. As would be seen a little later, this is mainly due to a large number of inmates belonging to 'Sudra' castes, including scheduled castes and scheduled tribes.

Religion as a variable shows little correspondence with other factors : most of the inmates are adherents of one religion, namely Hinduism. A few variations are seen in relation to the work assigned to the inmates. For example, about 77% of the Hindu inmates are engaged in trades, and about 19% of the Muslim inmates are doing maintenance work. Nevertheless, even these trends are not much dependable—statistical values are insignificant.

Caste : Among cognitive-structural attributes, a consideration of caste appears to be more important to the Indian social order than the religion. It is more so in view of the fact that most of the inmates in the jail under study are Hindus. For more than two thousand years, the institution of caste has been a dominant feature of the Indian social organisation. In the beginning, it was determined by *Karma* or deeds, but, as it obtains in contemporary times, it is decided by *Janma* or birth (see Prabhu, 1954). It is characterised by social stratification and hierarchy (Dumont, 1970). The caste system over the years has shown considerable resilience and adaptive capacity and has allowed a certain degree of vertical mobility as well (see Srinivas, 1966; Singh, 1973) Over 5000 castes, subcastes, and sub-subcastes are differentiated in terms of norms, customs, mores, taboos and the like. Needless to mention that these are in no way shed off while a convict enters the jail. They may persist and influence his thought, behaviour and amenability to correctional programmes.

Table 3.03 classifies inmates according to their caste. Although Sudra castes, sociologically speaking, include Scheduled Castes and Scheduled Tribes, they have been shown separately. Often regarded as the weaker sections of society, they

TABLE 3.03

Caste of the inmates

	Brahmin	Kshatriya	Vaishya	Kayastha	Sudra SC & ST	Others	Total
Frequency	44	44	06	01	176	66	337
Percentage	13.1	13.1	0.8	0 3	52.2	19.6	100.0

need to be focalised. It would be readily seen that more than half (52.2%) of the inmates belong to lower caste groups, namely Sudra, Scheduled Caste and Scheduled Tribes. Among the upper caste-groups, the preponderance is that of both Brahmins and Kshatriyas (13.1%). This notwithstanding, the majority of the inmate-population belongs to lower caste groups. Is it that they indulge in crime more than others ? Or, are they more easily identified and processed ?

Indeed, as a dominant social attribute, caste is linked with other inmate characteristics. For example, their educational status appears to vary with their caste ($p<.003$). As far as higher education, or to be specific; secondary education is concerned, Brahmins (34%) followed by Kshatriyas (20%) are seen to be in the forefront. This stands in sharp contrast with the fact that 60% of Sudras including Scheduled Caste and the Scheduled Tribes are illiterate. The trend that the caste and the educational status of the inmates are interlinked is confirmed by the statistics ($c=0.33100$). On the other hand, there is a clear case for strengthening the educational programmes in the institution, particularly for the inmates belonging to lower caste groups.

Interestingly, the use of intoxicants by the inmates and their caste show very little variation with each other. Alcohol and other habit-forming drugs seem to be popular with Sudra (53%) as also with Kshatriyas (13%). However, the use of chewing and smoking tobacco particularly that of *bidis* appears to be popular with all the inmates, whatever their caste. This may, in part, explain the significance of *bidis* in the jail life. Nevertheless, these variations are not much dependable—statistical values are far from being significant.

Caste appears to have little to do with the type or size of family the inmates come from. However, it does have some correspondence with some other familial aspects. The family educational status of the Brahmin inmates is high. Alternatively, the category 'educated families' is two-thirds made up of Brahmins and Kshatriyas; and that of 'illiterate families' is three-fourths made up of Sudras, Scheduled Caste and Scheduled Tribes ($p<.0035$; tau$=0.16607$; $p<.001$).

This is broadly in keeping with the findings on the education of the inmates ($p<.0003$). Family occupation also shows some notable variations ($p<.0001$). For instance, Brahmins are mostly engaged in agriculture and service; Kshatriyas, in agriculture ; Vaishyas, in business ; Sudra including Scheduled Castes and Scheduled Tribes, in agriculture and daily-wage work. These aspects need to be kept in view while organising work programmes in jails. The distribution of caste in terms of the family income of the inmates does not show significant differences. However, a mild trend is in evidence that Kshatriyas and Brahmins are somewhat better off than others (tau$= -0.06616$, $p<0.0382$).

Attention may now be shifted to offence-related variables. Caste of the inmates has a somewhat notable linkage with the offence for which they have been committed to the jail or with their being individual or group offender ($p<0.0348$). The distribution of relapse to crime or recidivism and the caste of the inmates is, however, not found to have any linkage with each other.

Has the caste of inmates anything to do with the work assigned to them in the jail ? The distribution of the data does not show any significant relationship with each other. But it would be observed that the proportionately more Brahmins are engaged in inmate-service including the jail kitchen, that more

Kshatriyas, in vocational training, and that more Scheduled Castes, in maintenance. The possibility can not be ruled out that caste is one of the consideration which weighs with the jail authorities while assigning work to the inmates.

Education : Directly relevant for the present purposes is the consideration of the educational background of the inmates. Education, in the words of Goldschmidt, is crucial to cultural mode of life (1960). As a means of enlarging the perception and experience of the individual, it may aid an inmate in adopting himself to the changed environment, as also help him in picking up new work skills (Khan and Unnithan, 1978). Illiteracy amongst the inmates, a discouraging feature in South-East Asian countries; and is reported to be a stumbling block in the implementation of correctional programmes (see Pillai, 1959). According to the official statistics the literacy rate in the State of Uttar Pradesh is 27.38%. The position obtaining at the Model Prison, Lucknow, is, however, a shade better (see Table 3.04). Only 47.5% of the inmates are illiterate and the rest are literate including about 13.4% who have received education up to secondary level or more. To a good deal, this feature of the jail population bids fair for the correctional programmes in the institution. However, the inmate-education may be looked into a little more closely.

Although the distribution of inmate-education in terms of their age is highly significant, the correlation between the two variables somewhat attracts the attention (tau= -0.07626; $p<.0180$). This partly suggests that young inmates are better educated than the older ones. A reference has already been

TABLE 3.04

Inmate education

	Illiterate	Primary	Secondary	Higher Secondary and above	Total
Frequency	160	102	30	45	337
Percentage	47.5	30.3	8.9	13.4	100.0

made to the correspondence between caste and education of the inmates. Brahmins followed by Kshatriyas appear to be better educated than Sudras and others. Similarly, type of family, that is, single or joint family ($p<.0622$) appears to vary with the inmate education. While the size of the family does not vary with this. Interestingly, the inmates coming from joint and large family groups appear to be relatively better educated. That inmate education and family educational status are correlated is amply brought out by the analysis ($c=0.67550$; $tau=0.67470$; $p<.0001$). On the other hand, family occupation is not significant, the correlation between the two variables attracts somewhat attention ($tau= -0.07973$; $p<.0165$). While the family income shows significant correspondence ($p<.0002$) with the education of the inmate. It is notable that the education of the inmates appears to be unimportant in relation to the offence they had committed whether singly or in groups and whether for the first time or otherwise. But it is significantly related to the work assigned to them in the prison ($p<.0004$).

Physical fitness : That the inmates should be provided safe and secure custody and that, towards this, they should have hygienic and healthy living conditions, has been a cornerstone of the prison policy in India, since long. More than a century ago the British Government had appointed a jail inquiry committee mainly to look into the mounting rate of sickness and death among the jail inmates. Likewise, the Indian Jail Committee (1919-20) has made pointed references to these aspects So has been the case with all the commission/committees and groups constituted by the central and state governments. Health and physical fitness of the inmates in jails assumes a pointed relevance in the present context : Work including vocational training is mainly for the health. This is what has been emphasised in the resolution of the First United Nations Congress on the Prevention of Crime and the Treatment of Offenders (1955); "all prisoners under sentence should be required to work subject to their physical and mental fitness...". Officially speaking, a thorough medical check-up of an inmate on entry is among the first procedure to be carried out. The inmate record called 'ticket' has elaborate columns for recording such details as height, weight and other physical and psychiatric particulars. In the jail under study, this record, however, has been found to be incomplete. It was difficult to generate data on the basis of information recorded on the tickets. In view of this, the choice has been for the assessment by the investigator. The inmates accordingly have been rated and classified in terms of their physical fitness (see Table 3.05). As would be seen from the table, more than three-fourths of the inmates are assessed to have average physical fitness and only 4.7% of them are, so to say, below average. To some extent, physical

TABLE 3.05

Inmates' physical fitness

	Below average	Average	Above average	Total
Frequency	16	268	53	337
Percentage	4.7	79.5	15.7	100.0

fitness is linked with the age in that older inmates are rated, by and large, to be more fit than younger inmates ($tau = -0.03487$; $p < 0.1689$; $c = 0.13185$). On the other hand, the physical fitness of the inmates also shows significant association with offence ($tau = -0.05443$; $p < 0.0673$). Physical fitness of the inmates is not linked with the nature of work which has been assigned to them in jail.

Marital status : A discussion of the marital status of the inmates is more than a formal necessity. This may in fact bring out whether antilegal behaviour is the consequence of social malintegration. Given this premise, most inmates in jails would be unmarried, divorced or separated. On the other hand, married inmates are likely to face adjustment problems in jails. Not only would they be denied conveniences of married life but also the thought of the plight of the spouse and other family members in their absence is likely to weigh them down. This may adversely affect their receptivity to correctional programmes.

TABLE 3.06

Marital status of the inmates

	Married	Widower/Separated/Divorced	Unmarried	Total
Frequency	262	26	49	337
Percentage	77.7	7.7	14.5	100.0

In the present sample (Table 3.06) more than three-fourths of the inmates, however, are married. While 7.7% of the inmates are widower including divorced or separated. Further, only 14.5% of them are unmarried. In a limited way, this shows that the inmates have not been necessarily maladjusted persons in their community. To what extent the married inmates have been sluggish in adjusting themselves with the life in the jail would be analysed a little later.

Who are the unmarried inmates ? Most of them are young people ($p<.0001$). Apparently, for a grownup to lead a married life is the norm. This trend cuts across all caste-groups and educational strata. Being married, of course, entails financial liabilities: In terms of per-capita family income, the unmarried inmates are somewhat better off than their married counterparts ($p<.0247$). Marital status and the use of psychotropic drugs are not found to be associated at all.

Vice-Level : There are many academicians and administrators who regard the use of intoxicating drugs as a contributory factor in criminal behaviour. Many have underlined the tendency of drug-users to indulge in crime particularly in property offences so as to maintain their habit. These issues are far from being settled. Patent, however, is the existence of organised crimes which underlay, the procurement, distribution and sale of psychoactive drugs both at the national and international levels. Besides, they may also have implications for the jail-life as well. Thomas (1977) reports that the response of the users of drugs and non-users to confinement differs significantly. Furthermore, drugs as mentioned earlier, form an important basis for the perpetuation of jail subculture.

In the preceding chapter, a brief reference to the use of intoxicants by the inmates has been made. Inmates have been penalised for the possession of narcotics. This, to some extent, has also been an issue of discord between them. Now an attempt may be made to enquire into the extent to which the inmates are given to such substances like chewing tobacco, smoking tobacco, alcohol, cannabis, opium and the like. Occasional or regular self-reported use of these by the inmates has been ascertained and a composite variable 'vice-level' has been coded. While doing so, the use of *pan* or betel leaves has been excluded. The inmates, who use two or more habit-forming substances regularly, have been coded as having high vice-level, those who use one substance regularly and two occasionally, as medium level, and the rest as low level. The distribution thus obtained is reflected in table 3.07. It would be seen that almost all of the inmates (99.6%) of the jail have a low vice-level. Beside this, 28.8% of the inmates are completely non-users. It may be added that the use of tobacco, canabbis and alcohol is farely widespread.

TABLE 3.07

Vice-level among the inmates

	High	Medium	Low	Total	NA
Frequency	—	1	239	337	97
Percentage	—	0.4	99.6	100.0	28.8

The data show that the use of intoxicants is not specific to age, religion, caste or educational status of the family, family occupation, income and marital status of the inmates or we can say, the use of drugs by the inmates appears to be independent with these familial aspects. Perhaps, the enthusiasm for drug cuts across all these groupings.

To some extent, the use of intoxicants by the inmates is seen to vary with the offence for which they have been imprisoned ($p<.0001$). Apparently, the use of habit forming drugs could be traced more to socio-cultural factors rather than to individual characteristics.

The above mentioned account relating to the personal characteristics of the inmates shows that to some extent their age and to a large extent their caste has been linked with the work which has been assigned to them in the jail. In this, even their physical fitness or educational status have had little or no place.

FAMILY BACKGROUND

In transmitting social norms and values from one generation to another and in shaping individual attitude and life scheme, the role of family has been generally recognised (see Freeman and Showel, 1957; Goode, 1959). Bogardus (1949) regards family as an informal school room of the human race. As a basic biological and social unit in society, it serves, among others, the function of schooling the children in the ideals and usages of the community of which it is a part. As an enduring association of interacting and intercommunicating personalities (Park and Burgess, 1924), it provides cultural continuity. It plays an incomparable role in the socialisation process of the individual (Whiting, 1963; Mintern and Lambert, 1964). Stated differently, much of the law-abiding or law-violating behaviour of a given individual could be traced to his family background. It is, therefore, hardly surprising that family has attracted considerable research attention in the etiomological studies of crime and delinquency.

The interaction and intercommunication between family members makes for what is termed a common culture. This process is found to be more pronounced in the Indian social context which has had a joint family system for centuries. The system has been under the pressure of several indigenous as well as exogenous forces but so far it has managed to survive particularly in rural areas. As is well known, a joint family has a greater generation depth, that is, three or more generations live together (Desai, 1943). It is a "group of people who generally live under one roof, who eat food cooked at one hearth, who hold property in common and who participate in common family worship and are related in some particular type of kindered' (Karve, 1953). The system has several advantages. It ensures cultural continuity, proper upbringing of children and security of individual members. However, it is not altogether free from limitations. It approximates and even abridges individual preferences, it rewards indolence and penalises dynamism and it promotes likes and dislikes 'in groups'.

It follows that the form and structure of family groups to a great extent affects individual members. Differences in family background, more often then not, are reflected in the subjective values, life scheme, social view and behavioural patterns of the individual. A study of a human grouping would hardly be complete without an analysis of the family background. Perhaps because of these considerations most studies focusing on inmates have concerned themselves with their family background (Clemmer, 1958; Sykes, 1958; Srivastava, 1977). With this in view, the composition, the educational and occupational status, economic condition, and criminality in the family the inmates in the present sample come from, are proposed to be looked into.

Size of the family : For several reasons, the size of the family may have a bearing on the conduct and behaviour of the individual members. The family groups which are small in size are often in a position to afford individual attention and to provide growth opportunities particularly to the youngsters. At the same time, they may unknowingly promote among the members a degree of individualism which may not necessarily conform to social norms. On the other hand, the family groups, which are large, provide a scope for varied interaction between the members. This may also make for a relatively greater social control. However, larger households often tend to be overcrowded—a phenomenon which does not augur well for social health. Against this backdrop, the size of the family of the inmates may be examined (see Table 3.08).

The data are inclusive of the inmate. It would be seen that about 65.5% of them come from small households, that is, having five members or less. The average size is found to be

TABLE 3.08

Size of the family of inmates

	Number of members in household				Total	NA
	3 and below	4-5	6-7	8+		
Frequency	72	137	73	37	337	18
Percentage	22.6	42.9	22.9	11.6	100.0	(5.3)

5.09 with negligible variance (standard deviation = 0.931). Perhaps, efforts directed at family planning in recent decades in the country have had some impact on the inmates' households as well. Has this also spawned individualism and nonconformity ? Size of the family, however, is not related to caste, the use of intoxicants, or the offence by the inmate. These positions may become a little clearer when the nature of family the inmates come from is examined.

Family composition : As mentioned earlier, the joint family system has been a distinctive feature of social organisation in India. These family groups, apart from greater generation depth, have several other features : Assets and liabilities are held in common, income earned by the members is pooled, and expenditure is incurred according to the need of a member irrespective of his earning. It has also been mentioned that the joint family system except in rural areas is fast vanishing. In the present context, an attempt has been made to ascertain the type of family the inmates come from. Towards this, only generation depth as ascertained through interview data has been relied upon and the type of the family of the inmates has been coded.

Table 3.09 presents the distribution. It would be seen that more than three-fourths of the inmates come from single family system or, in any case, from small households. This indicates that single family system has continued to be a feature of the social organisation. This is further reinforced by the fact that it is not specific to any caste-group : the two are more or less independent.

TABLE 3.09

Type of family of the inmate

	Single	Joint	Total	NR
Frequency	243	76	337	(18)
Percentage	76.2	23.8	100.0	(5.3)

Single family system may also provides for lesser social stability and social security. It follows that social responsibilities are met with less in single family (i.e. nuclear family) system than in joint family groups. This may be one of the reasons as to why the inmates coming from single family groups are better educated than others. The trend is confirmed by the high value of the correlation ($C=0.14984$; $p<0.0622$; $tau=0.12771$; $p<0.0003$). In keeping with the trend relating to the inmates' education, the educational status of the single family groups is also seen to be slightly higher than the joint family groups ($p<.0933$). While the main occupation in single family groups has been agriculture followed by service, it is service followed by business and labour in joint family groups. Also, the use of habitforming drugs is found to be relatively low among those from joint family ($tau=0.03553$; $p<.0121$). However, the inmates coming from single family groups are found to be economically better off than the others ($tau=0.08518$; $p<0.0114$). This is understandable : in large family groups, earnings get distributed yielding lower average income. The family composition also shows mild variations with the offence for which the inmates have been convicted ($p<0.0222$). To some extent, the data indicate that the members of the joint family groups may be more involved in a variety of disputes resulting in conflict, assault or even in murder and dacoity than the members of the single family groups.

Family educational status : Towards assessing general literacy and education in the family of the inmates, a composite variable family educational status has been generated. This takes into account the schooling and education of all the members in a household. When half or more family members have been reported to be graduates, it has been coded as highly educated, when half or more are matriculate, as educated; when atleast one member has done some schooling, as literate, and when no member is able to read or write, as illiterate. In the present sample, except for 18 inmates, all have offered information. The distribution is reflected in Table 3.10. It would be seen that majority of the inmates (58.0%) come from literate family groups and about 41.1% of them are from illiterate families. The proportion of those coming from educated family is indeed very small while none of the inmates belongs to highly educated family group.

TABLE 3.10

Family educational status of the inmates

	Highly educated	Educated	Literate	Illi-terate	Total	NR
Frequency	—	03	185	131	337	(18)
Percentage	—	1.9	58.0	41.1	100.0	(5.3)

The data indicate that Brahmin, Kshatriya as also some scheduled caste inmates come from are better educated families than others. However, this trend is not much dependable. Obviously, the family education is high in respect of those inmates who themselves are educated (tau=0.67470; $p<.0001$). The size of the family shows a good deal of relationship to the educational status ($p<.0933$). Apparently, small family groups have better educated members. On the whole, it may be remarked that negligible amount of inmates come from educated families and none of them come from highly educated families. This feature may not be specific to Lucknow, as a capital place of the Uttar Pradesh—it may be countrywide or even universal.

Family occupation : Quite a few researchers investigating crime and juvenile delinquency have paid attention to occupation. For example, Ferguson (1966) has reported that children coming from certain specific occupational groups are more likely to take to delinquent path. On the other hand, there are many others who have found little or no correlation between antisocial behaviour and occupation (Fleisher, 1966; McClintock, 1970). It would not thus take long to see that the scientific evidence in this regard is somewhat divided (Radzinowicz, 1971).

TABLE 3.11

Family occupation of the inmates

	Business	Service	Agri-culture	Labour	Total	NR
Frequency	17	08	284	10	337	(18)
Percentage	5.3	2.5	89.0	3.1	100.0	(5.3)

In coding family occupation of the inmates, the occupational pursuits of all the members in the household have been taken into consideration. In the case of a tie, family occupation has been decided on the basis of the main source of income, and, if the tie remained unresolved, on the basis of the occupation persued by the head of the household.

Table 3.11 presents distribution. It would be seen that majority (89%) of the inmates come from families engaged in agriculture; and another 3.1% from daily-wage earners. While only 5.3% of the inmates come from business family groups. That the inmate population is predominantly rural, would be readily seen.

Further analysis of data reveals that 52.2% of the inmates belonging to Sudras, including the inmates of Scheduled Castes, are almost evenly divided between agriculture and daily-wage work. On the other hand, Brahmins followed by Kshatriyas are over-represented in the service class. That inmates' education and family occupation are interlinked is to a good deal is brought out by the data (tau= —0.07973; $p<.0165$), of the illiterate inmates 46.1% are engaged in agriculture, and 70.0% in daily wage work. As would be expected, family occupation shows highly significant differences in terms of family educational status ($p<.0001$). The inmates who are from family groups with low educational status, their families are mostly engaged in agriculture and daily-wage work. Likewise, occupation seems to have a positive linkage with family earnings ($p<.0006$). Families of inmates engaged in business and agriculture appear to be better off than others. However, family occupation is not found having any correspondence with offence-related variables.

Family income : Since Baccaria, the nexus between economic status and criminality has attracted much research attention, although a consensus in this regard is yet to emerge (Orsagh and Witte, 1981). In any case, an attempt to look into the family earnings of the inmates may not be out of place. Table 3.12 presents the relevant data. It would be seen that about 55.3% of the inmates are from the families in which monthly income has been below Rs. 500. It indicates that majority of the inmates come from economically poor families. Only 20.9% of the inmates belong to economically good families whose total family earning is Rs. 1,000 per month and above.

TABLE 3.12

Total family income of the inmate (in rupees).

	—250	250—499	500—749	750—999	1000 +	Total	NR
Frequency	88	89	49	27	67	337	17
Percentage	27.5	27.8	15.3	8.4	20.9	100.0	5.0

The household income of the inmates shows good deal of relationship with the caste to which the inmates belong ($c=.26499$; $tau= -0.06616$; $p<0.0382$). At the same time, it shows for obvious reasons, a high correlation with family educational status; the families which enjoy high educational status also have large family income ($c=0.27973$; $p<.0007$; $tau= -023210$; $p<.0001$). Among the occupational classes, agriculture stands out ($p<.0006$) in that the families which are engaged in agriculture have relatively higher income. Furthermore, the data do not appear to vary with the offence committed by the inmates.

Further, the per capita family income of the inmates has been ascertained (see Table 3.13). This is likely to yield a relatively more reliable estimate (see Sjoquist, 1973). It would be seen that 51.4% of the inmates have a per capita income of less than Rs. 100 per month.

TABLE 3.13

Per capita family income of the inmates (in rupees).

	—50	50—99	100—149	150—199	200+	Total	NR
Frequency	81	83	50	33	72	337	(18)
Percentage	25.4	26.0	15.7	10.3	22.6	100.0	(5.3)

To some extent, per capita family income is found to be associated with the caste of the inmate (tau= —0.06292; $p<0.0463$). On the other hand, married inmates are relatively worse off ($p<0.0247$). As would be expected the inmates coming from single family groups have better per capita income.

Criminality in family : To the extent crime is a social phenomenon, the role of the family and familial environment on the law violating or law-abiding behaviour of individual members is critical. Should one or more members, particularly elderly members in a household, have criminal propensity or behaviour, it is likely to have an unsalutory impact on every member especially those who are tender in age. They may learn anti-social or criminal activities; their socialization may leave room for criminal behaviour or for a specific type of criminal behaviour; they may pick up criminal behaviour merely by imitating others; or else, they may accumulate law-violating definitions. A consideration of criminality in the family in a study of the present nature thus assumes a pointed significance.

To get at criminality in family, even in the case of those who have been committed to jail, is, however, fraught with several theoretical and practical difficulties. The existence of crime is a matter of formalism or lebelling, short of which it

TABLE 3.14

Criminality in the family of the inmates

	No	Yes	Total
Frequency	313	24	337
Percentage	92.9	7.1	100.0

may escape the attention of others, even of the family members. Further, many a person may not be candid about the criminal behaviour of their own family members.

However, in the present work there has been little scope for ascertaining criminality in family through means other than by asking the inmates themselves. Their responses are reflected in Table 3.14. Seemingly, only 7.1% of the inmates have had one or more members in their household given to criminal behaviour. Nevertheless, the possibility can not be ruled out that, owing to aforementioned reasons, the data may be suffering from respondent's bias. In any case, the data are too small for further analysis.

The criminality in family of the inmate shows a good deal of relationship with the caste; the inmates belong to ($p < .0024$). Taken together, it appears that inmates come from medium-sized family groups (average, 4-5 members to a household). Education in their households is not very popular : 41.1% of them are from illiterate households and 58% of them from those which are barely literate. Most of the inmates (92.1%) come from agricultural or agricultural labour families. Considering the rural character of the inmates-population, the family economic condition may not be regarded to be unsatisfactory; average household income is Rs. 374.5 per month and per capita income is Rs. 74.5. These aspects may well be kept in mind while considering the inmate population or their conduct and work in the jail.

CRIME AND SENTENCES

Crime detection, arrest, conviction and imprisonment all

these sequential events combine to make for a traumatic experience to the inmates in jail. This is likely to affect the course of their life and may have a direct bearing on their reformation and rehabilitation. Further, it has often been observed that correctional impact varies with the type of offence for which they have been imprisoned. For example, sexual offenders, drug traffickers and the like have been reported to be less amenable to change and modification in their behaviour (see for example, Glaser, 1964). Likewise, term of sentence may determine the level of their interest and participation in correctional programmes (Orland, 1975; Martinson, 1974). These are some of the dimensions which are proposed to be analysed.

Offence : Owing to the formalism built into the criminal law, offenders and hence inmates in jails, at times, are regarded as a homogenous group. However, this is seldom the case. Inmates in jails differ in many respects including in the nature and gravity of their offence. What is more, every inmate would represent a unique case should his intention, motives and deliberation or the circumstances are considered. A discussion of the nature of offence for which the inmates have been imprisoned, therefore, appears to be proper.

Among the reported offences, the bulk of the cases, according to the official statistics, relate to property offences including burglary, theft, pickpocketing, cattle, theft, bicycle-theft, anto theft, etc. These offences mostly carry short sentences of imprisonment. This often reflects on the composition of the inmate population in jails. However, probation laws are operative throughout the country which provide for release of an offender on probation, should he be young, first timer, and his offence less serious. This substantially reduces the proportion of property offender in the inmate population. This is what is brought out by the data presented in Table 3.15. It would be seen that the proportion of the inmates who have been committed to the jail for murder (81.3%) is the highest, followed by those, for dacoity. There is a very few of those who have been convicted for assault (4.5%).

Does offence vary with other factors ? Age of the inmates

TABLE 3.15

Offence of the inmates

	Assault	Murder	Robbery/ Dacoity	Total
Frequency	15	274	48	337
Percentage	4.5	81.3	14.2	100.0

shows enough correspondance with the offence inmates have committed (tau= −0.08831; $p<0.0076$). Caste of the inmate was also highly related with the offence committed by them (C= .23366; tau = 0.05394; $p<.0691$). Medical fitness of the inmates was also very significantly connected with the offence (tau= −0.05443; $p<.0673$). While other personal factors, like education, marital status, type of family and family occupation were more or less unrelated with this. The use of the intoxicants was also found to be significantly related to the nature of offence committed by the inmates ($p<.0001$). Those high in vice-level, were over-represented in the categories of assault and murder. As would be expected, 12.0% of inmates sentenced for dacoity/robbery were group-offenders. On the other hand, in the category of murder nearly 73.8% of the inmates were individual-offenders. In respect of such offences, variables like term of sentence, was highly significant with the offence (tau= −0.24284; $p<.0001$); and term left was also somewhat significantly related with the same (tau= −0.04728; $p<0.0969$). While the variable term served was more or less unrelated with the nature of the offence, the inmates who have committed murder, dacoity or robbery—carrying longer term of sentence—undergoing longer term in the jail and who still had larger term left, than others. It is worth noting that the nature of offence is significantly related to the work assigned to the inmates in the jail ($p<.0051$). The data shows that 84.9% of inmates, who were turned in for murder were allotted vocational trades. Further, among the convict officers, 66.8% were those who were convicted for homicide.

Recidivism : If the category of 'incorrigibles' was the centre of attraction in the nineteenth century, 'carrier criminals' are in contemporary times (Wilkins, 1969). However, to ascertain the recurrence of criminal behaviour is an uphill task (see Van der Werff, 1981). Detention, reporting and registration may be lackadaisical. Moreover, the present study has proceeded on the basis of official records and the information supplied by the inmates although both of these may not be complete or free from bias, Table 3.16 brings out that only two inmates in entire sample (337) inmates were a recidivists or repeater, which is very negligible.

TABLE 3.16
Recidivism among inmates

	First offender	Recidivist	Total
Frequency	335	02	337
Percentage	99.4	0.6	100

Individual/Group offence : Often, offences committed by a group of persons are considered to be pernicious and, hence, problematic from the standpoint of treatment. Ordinarily, such offences may have sub-cultural roots and the persons involved, instead, may be nursing a sense of injury. With this in view, the dichotomised information is presented in Table 3.17. It

TABLE 3.17
Individual and group offenders among inmates

	Individual offenders	Group offenders	Total
Frequency	84	253	337
Percentage	25.0	75.0	100

would be seen from the table that about three-fourths of the inmates are group offenders.

Committing an offence in group does not appear to be related to caste, education, use of intoxicants, term served, family income or the work assignment of the inmates. But age of the inmates is significantly related to this ($p<0.0136$).

This dimension corresponds with a wide variety of offence-related variables. The analysis shows that offences like murder or homicide have been having notable concentration of individual offenders, heinous offences like dacoity and robbery that of group offenders (tau = -0.06558; $p<.0362$), while murder is proportionate equal with both first and groups offenders. Beside, this, the data show that the two recidivists are reported to be group offenders. Furthermore, term of sentence is also significantly associated with the type of offender variable (tau=0.07891; $p<0.0153$), followed by slight variation of term left with this (tau=.04662; $p<.0007$). It would also be seen that the marital status of the inmates also shows a good deal of relationship with this (tau= -0.08326, $p<.0113$). At the same time, it presents, obviously, high correlation with the size of family (tau=0.19580, $p<.0001$) followed by type of the family (tau=0.07531; $p<0.0224$). Although type of offender does not vary with family income, as reported earlier, but the per capita income of the inmates is significantly associated with this (tau= -0.09295; $p<0.0066$).

Term of sentence : In relation to various correctional programmes, term of sentence of those committed to jail, has been often brought up. It is stated that short-termers remain practically untouched by various correctional programmes offered by the institution. On the other hand, the long-termers may take these programmes with indifference or even stoicism. Taken together, these considerations may give rise to scepticism as to the efficacy of the jail-system. This in view, the term of sentence the inmates were undergoing in the jail under study, may be looked into (Table 3.18).

It would be seen that majority of the inmates (86.6%) were in jail for sentences above ten years or life imprisonment which was followed by those (12.8%) who were sentenced for six to ten years. This suggests that the inmate population was made

TABLE 3.18

Term of sentence of the inmates (in years)

	3-5	6-10	Above 10 years and lifer	Total
Frequency	02	43	292	337
Percentage	0.6	12.8	86.6	100.0

up of mainly long-termers. This dimension may be examined a little further.

As would be the expectation, the term of sentence was closely associated with the nature of offence ($C=0.64571$; $p<.0001$); the inmates who had committed offences like robbery, dacoity and murder were undergoing larger terms of sentence. It is worth mentioning that this variable shows highly significant variations with the work assigned to the inmates in the jail ($p<0.0112$). To illustrate this, only 0.6% of the inmates who were undergoing a term of sentence of three to five years were assigned maintenance work. On the other hand, majority of the long-termers (6 years and above) were assigned to *karkhana* or factory. This would be discussed further a little later.

The above mentioned line of analysis has been persued further and the term served as also yet to be undergone of the inmates were examined (Table 3.19). It is observed that most of them are long-stayers to the institution in that nearly 20% of them were in it for a period of less than two years. In any case, about 47% of them have been in the jail for five years or more. Relatively long period of stay of the inmates in the jail also fits into the type of the institution under study.

As would be expected, the term served by the inmates has no linkage with their personal attributes. On the other hand, quite a few offence-related variables are relevant. For obvious reasons, term of sentence ($tau=0.12299$; $p<.0004$) and term-left ($p<.0765$) are highly correlated with term served by the

TABLE 3.19
Term served and left in the sentence of the inmates, in months (percentages).

	—6	7—12	13—24	25—60	61+	Total
Term served (N=337)	1.8	4.7	13.4	33.8	46.3	100
Term left (N=337)	—	0.6	1.5	8.6	89.3	100

inmates. Now, attention may be focused on the work assigned to the inmates and the time spent in the jail. The distribution was highly significant ($p < .0001$). Two features emerge sharp and clear : most of the inmates who were in the institution for two years and less (27%) were engaged in the maintenance work. On the other hand, most of those who had put in the jail more than five years (73.41%) were engaged in vocational trades. These data positions support the contention that newcomers were usually assigned to maintenance work and long stayers to vocational trades.

Next, attention may be turned to the term left in the sentence of the inmates (Table 3.19). It would be readily seen that about 98% of the inmates had more than two years term before their release from the institution. As mentioned earlier in case of term served, term left by the inmates also has no linkage with their personal characteristics. Only marital status has a good deal of relationship with the term left by the inmates ($p < .0053$). Relatively speaking, about 98% of the married inmates had two years or more to stay in the institution. Among offence-related variables, the trend corresponds with those presented earlier. The inmates who have been convicted for murder, followed by dacoity/robbery have still longer time to pass in the jail ($p < .0001$).

This dimension shows highly significant difference with the inmates' present work-assignment ($p < .0506$). The distribution of data closely follows the pattern outlined earlier; the inmates having left small terms are largely engaged in the maintenance work, while those having long-terms are in vocational trades.

All the three-variables—term of sentence, term served and term left—appear to be significant as far as the background of the inmates is concerned. Moreover, they have a significant bearing on the attitude and behaviour of the inmates, as would be seen a little later.

ROLE NORMS

Prison community has often been regarded a distinct normative structure (Holt, 1977). A kind of unwritten inmate code exists and is adhered to by most residents. This might govern their thinking and behaviour in almost all jail routines. Besides, inter-personal relations play a critical role. Based perhaps on reciprocated choices (Wellford, 1973), these linkages sustain and perpetuate jail subculture. Equally important in this connection is the institution of convict officers which is peculiar to India. Although from among inmates, they tend to make for a distinct group. If the process of prisonisation leads, among other things, to 'spiritual casteration' (Shallech and Berry, 1972), these convict officers may have no small hand in this. This aside, an average inmate is likely to embody the impact of these currents and cross-currents. Apart from this, his role perception is likely to be determined by these very forces. Earlier, an attempt has been made to delineate some of the subcultural aspects of the jail life which may now be examined in the light of the views expressed by the inmates.

Interpersonal Relations : The traumatic experiences through which inmates have undergone and the uncertainities they face during the early days in the jail may accentuate gregariousness and bring them closer. Whether this phenomenon occurs or not has been ascertained through interviews. Their responses are reflected in Table 3.20. That the inmates always help each other during crisis is affirmed by about 90.8% of the inmates. Indeed, they are speaking in the light of their own experiences. However, 2.7% of the inmates totally denied this. Therefore, there is a possibility that a section of the inmates, howsover small, does exist who are alienated. For this, there may be many reasons. The analysis, however, shows that the family

TABLE 3.20

Response of the inmates to the statement, "In time of need like illness, do you think that inmates help oiling person/inmates?"

	Never	Sometimes	Always	Total
Frequency	0.9	22	306	337
Percentage	2.7	6.5	90.8	100.0

economic condition of the inmates had mild relationship with this (tau=—0.04396; $p < .1199$). It is observed that inmates coming from middle income group were proportionately more positive about the fellow-feeling than those from lower and higher income groups. Besides, fellow feeling was significantly related to the size of the family (tau=0.06135; $p<0.0505$) and the age of the inmates ($p<.0243$).

In this very direction, an ideatory question has been posed to the inmates: do they live like members of a family ? Table 3.21 presents the responses; More than 91% of the inmates were positive about this, but quite a few expressed reservations. This partially shows that among inmates there were a few

TABLE 3.21

Response of the inmates to the question, "Do you feel that in the jail inmates live like members of a family?"

	No	Can't say	Yes	Total
Frequency	22	07	308	337
Percentage	6.5	2.1	91.4	100.0

inmates who were not able to adapt themselves to the life in jail. Indeed, such lack of adjustment may be traced to a variety of socio-cultural factors which may not be necessarily specific to the present setting. What is, however, specific to the social setting is the consideration of caste of the inmates.

As is well known, caste is both an association and institution. It incorporates unwritten but well defined rules governing approach, setting, commensalism, marriage and the like. On the other hand, the jail routine has little flexibility to respect caste-distinctions or to pander to caste-norms. For instance, not only do the inmates take meals together but also the meals are prepared in the community kitchen having hands belonging to different caste groups. Does this practice receive common approbation ?

TABLE 3.22

Response of the inmates to the question, "Do you approve the practice of serving meals to the inmates cooked by members of the different caste in the jail kitchen?

	No	Can't say	Yes	Total
Frequency	52	05	280	337
Percentage	15.4	1.5	83.1	100.0

Table 3.22 brings out that a vast majority of the inmates (83.1%) were concerned with caste norms relating to food and interdining and only 15.4% of them did not approve of this. As would be expected, the practice of serving meals to the inmates from the community kitchen was proportionately not much to the liking of the 'twice born' (Hutton, 1961) including Brahmins and Kshatriyas ($p<.0001$). Strangely enough, quite a few inmates belonging to Sudra (perhaps touchables) castes also did not favour this. On the other hand, inmates belonging to scheduled castes (mostly untouchables) and scheduled tribes did not mind the practice.

It can hardly be gainsaid that in a group situation interpersonal relations are characterised as much by understanding and cooperation as by disagreement and conflict. With this in view, an attempt has been made to explore the latter (Table 3.23). A sizable section of the inmates (23.1%) reported that sometimes inmates did quarrel with each other, followed by 1.5% of them who reported that inmates always did so.

TABLE 3.23

Response of the inmates to the question, "In your opinion, do inmates quarrel with each other ?"

	Never	Sometimes	Always	Total
Frequency	254	78	05	337
Percentage	75.4	23.1	1.5	100.0

Interestingly, in reporting this, the age of the inmates showed a good deal of relationship with the inmates' conflict (tau= 0.07032; $p<0.0266$). It is supported by the significant variation of term served (tau=—0.08836; $p<.0076$). Inmates' conflict was also closely associated with the fellow feelings (tau=—0.13953; $p<.0001$). Use of intoxicants by the inmates appeared to be unrelated with this.

The above mentioned line of enquiry has been pursued further and an attempt was made to ascertain the frequency of

TABLE 3.24

Inmates' response to the question, "How many times had it (inmate quarrel) happened during the last month ?"

	Severally	Occasionally	Once/ Twice	Not at all	Total	NR
Frequency	03	31	26	24	84	253
Percentage	3.6	36.9	31.0	28.6	100	(75.1)

the inmate quarrel during the month preceding the interview (Table 3.24). It would be seen that a sizable section of inmates reported these conflict situations. In this, those who were in the jail for long periods out proportion others (p<0.0411).

While on this, an attempt may be made to look into the issues giving rise to conflicts among the inmates. The range of issues is as wide as it is interesting (Table 3.25). It would be seen that more than half (58.3%) of the inmates reports that due to abusing or loose talk, conflict between the inmates

TABLE 3.25
Showing the issues of conflict among the inmates

	Old enemity	Abuse/ loose talk	Stealing garments & other material	Work	Total
Frequency	03	35	16	06	60
Percentage	5.0	58.3	26.7	10.0	100

occurs. Besides, a sizable section of inmates (26.7%) reports that smoking tobacco including bidis appears to be so much in demand as to impel many inmates to resort to stealing. So might be the case with the items issued to the inmates including garments.

Do these conflict issues differ with other inmate characteristics? The age of the inmates was found to be relevant (tau=.15324; p<.0390). It was supported by the personal variables, like marital status of the inmates with significant variations (tau=— 0.20667; p<.0087); and education of the inmates (tau=—0.14569; p<0.0470). Likewise in this, family economic condition also appeared to be very closely related to the conflict issues among the inmates (tau=—0.23638; p<0.0041). It would also be seen from the analysis of data that the caste of the inmates was not relevant to the issue. On the whole, inmate conflicts, whatever the frequency or issues, appeared to be an inseparable feature of life in the jail.

Convict officers : To the range of interpersonal relationship, the practice of having convict officers in jails added yet another dimension. As mentioned earlier, they were appointed from among the inmates to serve as a link between them and jail authorities. They did not get any remuneration but were allowed a few benefits and privileges. In the main, they were supposed to assist authorities in the day-to-day administration and to help the inmates in a variety of ways. Keeping this backdrop in view, an attempt was made to ascertain the view-point of the inmates.

According to the U.P. Jail Manual, convict officers—including convict watchman, convict overseer and convict warders—were supposed to be well-behaved and industrious. Table 3.26 brings out relevant information regarding the perception of the inmates of the criterion used in such appointments. It would be seen that more than 95% of the respondents go along the official criteria; but there are also those who refer to certain extraneous considerations. There is a solitary case of a respondent reporting that even mischief mongering could lead to appointment. The distribution shows few variations with inmate characteristics.

TABLE 3.26

The response of the inmates to the question, "What is the most important consideration in getting appointment as convict officer?"

	Term served	Conduct record	Money	Impression on authorities	Education	Mischief mongering	Total
Frequency	223	52	02	02	01	01	281
Percentage	79.4	18.5	0.7	0.7	0.4	0.4	100

Convict officers are allowed some additional remission which may vary according to their grade. This apart, they may manage a few other benefits and privileges. In this respect, the views of the inmates were assessed (Table 3.27). Remission stands out as the most important advantage the convict officers have about 72.6% of the respondents mention it. Nonetheless a few off the record advantages also showed up. It may be noted that a few inmates mention that convict officers do not have to work, a fact which is not strictly in keeping with the rules.

TABLE 3.27

Response of the inmate to the question, "In your opinion what is the most important advantage one has as convict officer ?"

	Remission	Status	Food	No work	Medical	Total
Frequency	204	04	18	54	01	281
Percentage	72.6	1.4	6.4	19.2	0.4	100.0

Next, attention may be paid on inmate-convict officer relationship. A reference to this dimension has already been made in Chapter II (Table 2.09). It has been pointed out that in the opinion of 11.4% of the inmates, convict officers behaved with other inmates in a rather authoritative manner. Quite a few of them (2.8%) reportedly, acted as bosses. To some extent, these negative aspects were neutralised by the presence of the convict officers who were understanding and helpful. Interestingly, the opinion of the inmates about their relationship with the convict officers tended to vary with some personal variables, like caste of the inmates (tau=—0.07387; $p<0.0319$); education of the inmates also showed relevant variation with this (tau=—0.09851; $p<0.0067$). Furthermore, the economic condition of the inmates showed good deal of association with the convict officers-inmates relationship (tau=0.09632; $p<.0096$). Inmate convict officers relationship also reflected their relevance to the term served by the inmates (tau=—0.10077; $p<0.0057$).

Attention has been focused on the role played by convict officers during interviews. In the preceding section it has been found that, in the opinion of more than half (56.8%) of the inmates, convict officers are unhelpful in arranging interview with their visitors. Again, the use of intoxicants by them shows slight variation with this aspect ($tau=0.05693$; $p<0.0968$). Likewise, it has also been ascertained whether convict officers excise gifts which inmates receive during interview. Almost all of them are negative in this regard, while there is a solitary case of a respondent reporting affirmatively.

Inmate-convict officer conflict is yet another point which may be brought into focus. A detailed reference to this has already been made in Chapter II (Table 2.12). A sizable section of the inmates (16.4%) reported that convict officer did get displeased with them. A few of the inmates reported the occurrence of these situations during the month preceding data collection. Since this dimension shows significant variation with the age of the inmate ($tau=0.16749$; $p<0.0327$), the existence of these conflict situations seems to be real and frequent. Such conflicts had many underlying issues including discipline, work, flattery and the like. Notably, first-timers gave a normative response : convict officers got angry with inmates for disciplinary reasons; but the recidivists thought otherwise. Needless to add, many inmates crossing the path with convict officers faced unsavoury consequences.

For the last sixty years or so the practice of having convict officers has constantly been a target of severe criticism. In the opinion of knowledgeable circles, this practice has done to the institutional objectives far more harm than good.

Role perceptions : Lastly, attention may be focused on the roles inmates saw for themselves in the jail. It may be pointed out that this dimension was as important as it was difficult to ascertain. Interview questions or items have necessarily to be ideatory and may tend to get normative response. This is what would be generally noticed on going through data presented in Table 3.28. An overwhelming majority of the inmates was aware of their role vis-a-vis jail authorities. Adherence to these role norms may, of course, be a different story. Nonetheless, a few variations were observed when it came to working without bothering about remission or reward; on improvement of ideas and conduct, one out of ten inmates expressed reservations. However, the possibility can not be ruled that the data suffer from respondents' bias. Perhaps these dimensions need to be explored using some other technique.

TABLE 3.28

Response of the inmate to Role norm statements (percentage).

Statement	Not impor-tant	Somewhat important	Impor-tant	Total
"Is it important to you to keep warder and jail authorities happy or is it not important to you ?	8.1	3.9	88.0	100
"Is it important to you to complete sentence giving jail authorities no occasion to get displeased ?	2.4	4.5	93.0	100
"Is it important to you to work hard without bothering about remission or reward ?"	8.1	4.2	87.8	100
"Is it important to you to use the time in jail towards improving your ideas and conduct ?"	2.4	4.5	93.2	100

Optimism : It can hardly be contested that inmates' view of life in jail was a critical factor. An inmate who had a positive and optimistic attitude was likely to face fewer problems of adjustment in the near regimented ambience and with the officials or fellow residents. Similarly, his conduct and behaviour was likely to be more acceptable to all concerned. What was more, he would relatively be more interested and participative in correctional programmes offered by the institution. It follows that he would benefit more than others from these, including work programmes, leading to positive changes in his thinking and behaviour. With these considerations in view, the opinion of the inmates in the present sample was elicited on a hypothetical issue : Do they think that the life in jail in the days to come would be happier than what it was. Their responses are presented in Table 3.29. It would be seen that nearly three-fourths of them agreed with the statement and thought that a better future for them lay ahead. Nevertheless, there does remain a sizable section of theirs (18.7%) which is pessimistic or undecided about it.

The analysis of the data brings out that this kind of optimism-pessimism is somewhat related to the economic condition of the inmates ($p<0.0598$). Seemingly, the process of prisonisation gradually dampens enthusiasm resulting in stoicism

TABLE 3.29

Response of the inmate to the statement, "Certain recent changes in government policy concerning jail working promise a better future for the inmate."

	Disagree	Can't say	Agree	Total
Frequency	24	63	250	337
Percentage	7.1	18.7	74.2	100.0

or pessimism. Notwithstanding this, correctional programmes could do much to elevate sagging spirits. Should these be interesting and purposive, they would also boost up the inmates. This is what is brought out by the analysis. The inmates who were engaged in vocational trades and inmate service had much positive attitude ($tau=0.05626$; $p<0.0720$). It was followed or further highly supported by the variable of achievement scale in vocational training ($p < 0.0375$) rated by the instructors.

Towards assessing capability of the inmates for work programmes, their personal attributes, family background, offence and role norms have been looked into. Taken together, an average inmate in the jail under study was a youngish male Hindu and belongs to some so-called lower caste-group. He would be illiterate or at best primary educated. Physically fit and married, he would be given to habit-forming drugs specially *bidi*, chances are that he is from a slightly large joint family which would be illiterate and engaged in agriculture with reasonably adequate income. The possibility was that he was for the first time involved in the offence of murder or dacoity perpetrated conjointly with others. Undergoing a term of imprisonment of more than five years, he was an affable person ready to help others in their hour of need like a family member. Occasionally, he picked up quarrel with a fellow inmate or convict officer.

The foregoing thumb-nail sketch underlines that the suitability of an average inmate to different work programmes in the jail was a mixed package. His literacy level was not much encouraging; he harboured caste feelings and was involved in some serious offences. Contrariwise, he is young and physically fit. He cannot be termed 'hardened'. Since the offence has been committed in group, he may not have a wholly despoiled nature. Furthermore, he is relatively a long-termer for whom programmes can be planned. All things considered, the hypothesis is only partially supported.

4

The Personnel

At the outset, a mention may be made to the insight-stimulating accounts provided by the prison administrators themselves (Brockway, 1912; Osborne, 1928). Besides, Shelleck and Berry (1972), Holt (1977) and several others have analysed prison management and related aspects. Verin (1973), Peretti and Hooker (1976) have in the main concerned themselves with the custodial staff. While Ponti and Sacchi (1975) emphasize on staff training, Holder (1978) underlines human resource development. Delineating the staff-inmate relationship, two focused studies may be mentioned. These are by Brown et. al., (1971) and by Riscalla (1975). Murton (1976) has been rather critical of prison personnel and has grouped them into six categories : the Neophyte, the Careerist, the Warrior, the Therapist, the Curator, and the Diplomat. Needless to add that the studies referred to above directly or indirectly also evaluate the background, equipment and performance of the correctional staff. That the field of correctional service is unattractive, offers inadequate incentives, has indifferent working conditions and enjoy low public prestige, has also been underlined in the Task Force Report, 1967.

The foregoing account shows that systematic and focused literature on prison personnel, their background and capabilities, their problems and prospects, their identification with and commitment to job, and the like is precious little. This kind of paucity of literature is more so acute in relation to the Indian context. Motivated by the above mentioned considerations, in this section it is proposed to focus on the staff in the jail under study. Towards this, it examines the hypothesis : "*The custodial as well as vocational staff are sufficiently oriented in the reformatory ideals*". Towards this, personal aspects, professional background, job satisfaction, role identification and staff culture have been enquired into. It may be added that attention has been paid only to custodial and treatment staff; (2—3 office/administrative functionaries have been precluded from the sample). Again, since the number of vocational instructors in the jail is too small to form a meaningful statistical category, their responses have been used only as case material.

PERSONAL ASPECTS

It has often been brought out that the institutional staff has a perceptible impact on inmates (see, for example, Galway, 1948; Moran, 1954). To what extent this impact would be therapeutic and correctional would depend much upon the personal characteristics of the functionaries, including their age, religion, education, caste etc. As such, some of the prominent personal aspects may be looked into.

Age : The better part of the work in correctional institutions is a helping activity which makes heavy demands on the understanding as well as the maturity of the practitioners. Stated differently, the practitioners who are mature in age would be in a better position to exercise a meaningful and positive influence on the residents. A perusal of Table 4.01 would show

TABLE 4.01

Age of the staff members. (in years)

	—25	25—35	35—45	45—55	55+	Total
Frequency	02	14	36	58	10	120
Percentage	1.7	11.7	30.0	48.3	8.3	100

that majority of staff (90%) of the staff is in the age group of 25—55 years; and very few are below 25 years in age while there is a sizable section (8.3%) of the staff who are above 55 years of age. Partly, this age distribution could be attributed to the age limits laid for entry and superannuation (18 and 58 years, respectively). That most of the staff members are mature in age is also underlined by their mean age of 45 years with a fairly normal distribution (SD=8.6 years).

As would be expected, age of the staff members and their job experience are mutually correlated (tau=0.59602; $p<.0001$), that is to say, the officials who are old have also put in many years in service. Yet another aspect which attracts attention is the fact that the treatment staff as also vocational staff is some what older than the custodial staff (tau= —0.12241; $p<.0227$). Since it is the treatment and vocational staff which is directly responsible for carrying out the correctional programme, their maturity in age augurs well.

Religion and Caste : Religious affiliation does not merely represent one's faith in the unknown, it also denotes his way of life. Depending upon the stimulus and situation, it may greatly influence his thinking and behaviour. At times, it may have a critical role in shapping his predispositions or prejudice. Keeping this in view, the religious affiliation of the staff members has been ascertained (see Table 4.02).

TABLE 4.02

Religion of the staff members

	Hindu	Muslim	Sikh	Total
Frequency	106	13	01	120
Percentage	88.3	10.8	0.8	100

It would be readily seen that the most of the staff members (88.3%) belong to Hindu religious group, while a sizable section (10.8%) of the staff members belongs to Muslim community.

In the Indian social context, the dimension of caste is often regarded to be more important than religion. Further, within the broad Sudra group, Scheduled Castes and Scheduled Tribes have been statutorily marked for selective upliftment. As is known, there are reservations in educational institutions and services and representation in legislatures. With this fact in view, the caste of the staff members may be examined. On going through Table 4.03, it would be seen that 39.2% of the staff members are Brahmins and 18.3% of Kshatriyas. All other caste groups, including Scheduled Caste and Scheduled Tribes, are somewhat underrepresented. A comparison of this with the

TABLE 4.03

Caste of the staff members

	Brahmin	Kshatriya	Vaishya	Kayastha	S.C.	S.T.	Others	Total
Frequency	47	22	05	11	14	01	20	120
Percentage	39.2	18.3	4.2	9.2	11.7	8.0	7.6	100

data presented in Table 3.03, on the caste of the inmates, may not be out of the place. Nearly 42.5% of the inmates belong to lower caste groups; as against this, only 12.5% of the staff members came from these caste groups. It would be also seen from the analysis of data that the caste of the staff member varies with the functional branch of the staff members (tau= 0.0885; $p<0.0740$) as also with their functional status (tau= 0.15583; $p<.0054$). This fact may have a bearing on the staff-inmate relationship in the jail.

Marital status and dependents : Familial responsibilities may be expected to determine the satisfaction which a functionary may have from his job. It is from this angle that the marital status and the number of dependents of the staff members become important. It is found that among them only two are unmarried, 3.3% are widower and the rest (95%) are married. As far as the number of dependents are concerned (see Table 4.04), most of them (97.5%) have three or more dependents. It

TABLE 4.04

Dependents of the staff members

	Not applica-ble	2 depen-dents	3—5 depen-dents	5+ depen-dents	Total
Frequency	1	2	54	63	120
Percentage	0.8	1.7	45	52.5	100

would be justifiable to say that they have marginally large household to maintain. This dimension along with incentives may have a linkage with their level of job satisfaction.

Education : The jail system is as much a formal organisation as it is intricate. It is, therefore, hardly surprising that it makes heavy demands on those who man it. Among other things, it requires a level of formal education. It may be pointed out that previously formal education, particularly among the lower rungs of official, was not much emphasized. However, with the increase in the literacy level and proliferation of education, the situation has undergone a marked change. In the state, the minimum educational qualification for the recruitment to the post of warder is matriculation/higher secondary, of the Assistant Jailor, graduate and of the Jail Superintendent, post-graduate. Nevertheless, there would be, among staff members, many old-timers who would not be well off as far as formal education is concerned.

Table 4.05 brings out that majority (80%) of the staff

TABLE 4.05

Education of the staff-members

	1—5	5—8	8—11	U.G.	P.G.	Total
Frequency	09	15	65	15	16	120
Percentage	7.5	12.5	54.2	12.5	13.3	100

members are educated above the eighth standard, including graduation (12.5%) and post-graduation (13.3%). Taken together, the staff members are better off educationwise.

Formal education of the staff in jail somewhat related with the prior experience in jail service ($p<0.0338$). It is also supported by the functional status ($tau=0.14722$; $p<0.0081$) and functional branch ($tau=0.14722$; $p<.0081$) of the staff. Furthermore, it is closely associated with the length of service of the staff ($tau= -0.41128$; $p<.0001$), that is to say, not only is the supervisory and intermediate staff highly educated but also some of the subordinate staff have graduate degrees.

PROFESSIONAL BACKGROUND

That jail functionaries should have proper aptitude, educational background and job training has been greatly emphasized (see, for example, the U.S. Presidential Commission on Law Enforcement and Administration of Justice, 1967, p. 175). A few have gone to the extent of comparing jail professionals with business executives. "It will be necessary", observe Ponti and Sacchi, "to form a new generation of prison directors by the same principles as those used to give business managers technical, professional as well as psychosocial training" (1975). In order to examine professionalism among the staff members, their job training, length of service, functional status, etc., have been analysed.

Job training : The human resources development (HRD) model has been very popular in an industry and with business corporations. On a selective basis, the HRD model has also been experimented in a few jail settings (Holder, 1978). The assumption has been that the staff can be systematically selected and trained first to learn new skills themselves and then to deliver them to residents. Reportedly, it has also helped in curbing recidivism. Not much thought has been paid to the HRD in the Indian context. Nonetheless, with a view to securing a systematic understanding, wherewithal meant to help and reform the inmates of jails, prior experience and the job training of the staff members may be examined. A perusal of

Table 4.06 would reveal that a very negligible proportion of the staff members (2.5%) had any worthwhile experience prior to their joining jail service. As a matter of fact, about 97.5% of them had little by way of prior experience. It is relevant to mention that prior experience is found to be closely linked with the functional status of the staff members ($p<0.0021$). For example, 97. 8% of subordinate staff had no prior experience against only 2.2% of them who had some prior experience; none of the intermediate staff; and only one of the supervisory staff had substantial experience before their joining jail service. Supervisory staff, in terms of prior experience, is better off than

TABLE 4.06

Prior experience of the staff members.

	No training	Some training	Substantial training	Total
Frequency	117	03	—	120
Percentage	97.5	2.5	—	100

subordinate and intermediate staff. What is, however, relevant is job training. Granted that men of aptitude, requisite background and educational qualifications would be available, they have to be oriented to the job. It is, therefore, in the fitness of things that training is emphasised in almost all walks of human activity. It may be noted that the state has a Jail Training School at Lucknow, which is very near to the jail under study, providing induction or refresher training for the jail personnels of all categories. In either case, it is not deemed necessary first to provide foundation or induction training and then put a person on the job. More frequently than not, a person after undergoing a selection procedure may join his post and may take up a training programme, later depending upon the convenience of the department and often times of his own. This is what is revealed by the data presented in Table 4.07. Despite Jail Training School near by the jail under study, a majority of the officials (88.3%) have received no job training whatsoever. This hardly bids fair for the jail functioning. It is also relevant to mention that job training is found to be significantly associated with the functional branch (tau=0.16792; p<.0030). It is strongly supported by the functional status of the staff (tau=0.24323; p<.0001). That the vocational staff in terms of job training would be better off than custodial staff of the jail is understandable.

TABLE 4.07

Job training of staff members

	No training	Some training	Substantial training	Total
Frequency	106	07	07	120
Percentage	88.3	5.8	5.8	100

Length of Service : While discussing personnel aspects, it is customary to emphasise on job experience. Perhaps experience enables a functionary to have a better grasp of the job requirements and acquit himself from the responsibilities better. Nevertheless, in a dynamic organisation, long years of service may also be a drag, should the functionary be tardy in adapting himself to changed conditions. These issues have presumably a pointed relevance to the jail organisation.

A glance on Table 4.08 would show that most of the staff members have put in several years of service in the jail organisation. To be precise, about three-fourths of the staff members have been in the jail organisation for a decade or more. This trend is further supported by the average of 15 years.

TABLE 4.08

Length of service of staff members (in years).

	−5	5—10	10—20	20—30	30+	Total
Frequency	03	27	58	21	11	120
Percentage	2.5	22.5	48.3	17.5	9.2	100

It would also be seen from the data that the length of service is closely associated with the functional branch (tau= —0.19685; p<0.0006). It is highly linked with the functional status of the staff (tau=—0.17521; p<.0021). This shows that the intermediate and subordinate functionaries have been in the jail service relatively for long years. Besides, it is related with their educational background, in an interesting way. There is a strong but negative correlation between the two (tau= —0.41128; p<0.0001), indicating that juniors have better formal education than seniors.

Staffing pattern : The staffing pattern in the jail could have been brought under discussion earlier but for a few methodological reasons. In Chapter II, a reference has already been made to functional positions in the jail. Now a few other related aspects may be highlighted.

In view of the emphasis on treatment, reformation and rehabilitation of offenders the ratio between custodial and treatment staff calls for a review. For the purposes of analysis, the staff members interviewed have been grouped. Table 4.09 presents staff members according to their functional branch.

TABLE 4.09

Functional branch of the staff members

	Custodial	Non-Custodial	Vocational	Unclassified including educational	Total
Frequency	97	03	09	11	120
Percentage	80.8	2.5	7.5	9.2	100

Functional branch of the staff has very significant variations with their length of service (tau=—0.19685; p<.0006) in a very interesting way. That custodial staff has been in jail service relatively for long years than vocational staff of the jail.

While on this, attention may also be paid to the functional status of the staff members. A reference to Table 4.10 would show that three functionaries have been classified as having supervisory status, including Superintendent, Deputy Superintendent and out of two-one Senior Jailor; twentyfour functionaries, such as one Junior Jailor, 5 Deputy Jailors, 8 Assistant Jailors, Doctors etc., as having intermediate status; and the rest as having subordinate status. As would be expected, the education of the Supervisory and intermediate functionaries is significantly better than the subordinate staff ($p<.C001$). As would also be seen a little later, these dimensicns, namely,

TABLE 4.10

Functional status of the staff members.

	Subordinate	Intermediate	Supervisory	Total
Frequency	93	24	03	1 0
Percentage	77.5	20.0	2.5	100

functional branch and functional status have a bearing on the preferences of the staff members ($C=0.43338$; $tau=0.20187$; $p<0.0005$). For example, more than eightyfive per cent of subordinate functionaries are custodial; and out of three supervisory functionaries, two belong to custodial staff.

STAFF CULTURE

If the inmates in a jail make for a sub-culture, so might be the case, in varying degrees, with staff members. Generally speaking, the nature of inter-functionary communication and relationship, role-models and so forth are the likely subcultural parameters A prominent few may be focalised, here.

Communication: It hardly needs a mention that correctional institutions are goal-oriented service organisations having little resembelance with the Weberian model. Rigidly defined, hierarchy and impersonal working are unlikely to be conducive to the realisation of correctional objectives. This is where interfunctionary communication assumes a pointed significance (see also Glaser, 1971; Duffee, 1975). Needless to add, free-flowing communications would greatly strengthen the problem-solving process in the institution and engender comaradrie amongst the staff members. Towards ascertaining this dimension, they have been asked as to how often they have discussed

TABLE 4.11

Responses of the officials to the question, "During the preceeding month concerning your job/work how often did you talk with the following?" (Percentage)

	Severally	Occasionally	Once or Twice	Not at all	Total
Superiors (N=120)	05	60.8	1.7	32.5	100
Colleagues (N=120)	7.5	78.3	—	14.2	100

their professional problems with their superiors and colleagues. Their responses are reflected in Table 4.11. Even though the stimulus is highly generalised, the responses are revealing. For example, 32.5% of the officials, have never discussed their functional problems with their superiors. Perhaps hierarchial functioning in the jail is pervasive. Lateral communications between the colleagues is a shade better, but even here there are officials (14.2%) who had no occasion or who did not find any need to discuss their professional problems with colleagues. Taken together, both formal and informal channels of communication in the different rungs of the jail organisation need to be smoothened.

Subordinate-Superordinate relationship : The dichotomy of hierarchial and lateral functioning may be pursued further by looking into the nature of subordinate-superordinate relationship. The officials have been asked whether their superiors are harsh, indifferent or considerate in supervising their work (the presentation of data is deferred) that the question raised is somewhat ego-hurting would be noticed. Nevertheless, 10.8% of the officials state that their superiors are strict to the extent of being harsh. As against this, 57.5% of them feel that their superiors are considerate. The above line of analysis has been probed further. The data presented in Table 4.12 bring out superiors' attitude towards the subordinates as perceived by the latter. It would not take long to see that on the whole officials are not well disposed towards their superiors; the frequency of the negative responses in respect of all four questions is larger than of positive responses. This becomes more obvious in regard to subordinate-superordinate consultation. About 95.8% of the

TABLE 4.12

Superiors' attitude as perceived by the officials (Percentage)

	Never	Sometimes	Always	Total
Do your superiors praise you when you do satisfactory work ?	71.7	12.5	15.8	100
Do superior officers try to solve the problems of the jail officials rather than find fault with them ?	10	3.3	86.7	100
Do your superiors consult you before making changes in the routines concerning your work field ?	95.8	4.2	—	100
To what extent are superior officers willing to listen to the problems of subordinate officers.	28.3	66.7	5	100

officials report that their superiors never consult them before making changes in their routine concerning their field. This kind of consultation is significantly related to the educational level of the officials ($p < .0002$). Interestingly, this kind of consultation appears to be relatively more in treatment branch than in custodial branch ($p<.0001$). On the whole, superiors' attitude in the institution belies a hierarchical approach.

In an open-system, characterised by two-way communications and healthy subordinate-superordinate relationship, opinions on professional issues would be expressed freely. This may provide an important feedback and may help in readjusting organisational programmes. In order to assess this dimension, an attempt was made to ascertain the extent and nature of disagreement of the officials with their superiors. A reference to Table 4.13 would show that very few members of the staff disagreed with their superiors (4.2%). Majority of those (95.8%)

TABLE 4.13

Responses of the officials to the question, "Concerning your job/work you do at times disagree with your superiors ? If yes, how often did it happen during the last month ?

	Severally	Occasionally	Once or twice	Not at all	Total	NA
Frequency	—	03	02	—	05	115
Percentage	—	60	40	—	100	(95.8)

who did not agree with their superior, out of which 60% of them occasionally disagreed and 40% reported to have disagreed once or twice during the preceeding month, with their superiors. What were the main issues of disagreement ? Only five officials offered information on this. They reported miscellaneous issues, extra or irregular duties, and the household work at the jail officers' residence. It may be noted that disagreement with the superiors did not necessarily imply a formal disagreement. Even then, a vast majority of the officials were non-responsive. This aside, the issues, though reported by a small number of officials, were disquieting.

Successful Officers : The significance of imitation models in individual or organisational behaviour can hardly be discounted. It is easy to suggest that the working of the officials perceived to have a successful career would be in varying degrees emulated by others. It would, therefore, be relevant to find out as to what are the traits of the most successful officer in the jail, as perceived by the officials. Keeping the above in view, the response pattern of the officials may now be examined (Table 4.14). The distribution of the data is highly revealing. Should we focus on the positive aspects of the traits and on the last three columns in the table, the picture of the most successful jail officer which emerges is something like this. In the first place

TABLE 4.14

Response of the officials to the questions, "In your opinion who is the most successful officers in this jail ?"

(Percentage)

Traits	1	2	3	4	5	Total
Ignorant—Knowledge (N=120)	—	1.7	—	5	93.3	100
Unconcerned about inmates —Concerned (N=120)	2.5	4.2	3.3	0.8	89.2	100
Inefficient—Efficient (N=120)	2 5	16.7	3.3	0.8	76.7	100
Lazy—Hard working (N=120)	2.5	17.5	3.3	—	76.7	100
Corrupt—Honest (N=120)	2.5	10	29.2	—	58.3	100
Does not cooperate with colleagues—Cooperates (N=120)	68.3	25	2.5	3.3	0.8	100
Shaky—Bold (N=120)	—	1.7	5	19.2	74.2	100
Strict—Considerate (N=120)	2.5	1.7	10.8	11.7	73.3	100

he should be knowledgeable (jail rules, regulations, etc.); and secondly, he should be concerned with the problems of inmates in the jail. In the third place, he should be efficient in his working and on the fourth place, he should be bold in his actions. Besides, he should also be honest and concerned with the jail-machinery and for the welfare and reformation of the inmates, and also with the functionaries.

Unsuccessful Officer : It would not be without interest to ascertain the point of view of the official converse to the above. As such, the traits of the most unsuccessful jail officer as perceived by the officials have been ascertained (Table 4.15). In their assessment, the image of the most unsuccessful officer, which comes up, shows that he is a strict and lazy person who does

TABLE 4.15

Response of the officials to the question, "In your opinion who is the most unsuccessful officers in this jail?" (Percentage).

Traits	1	2	3	4	5	Total
Does not cooperate—Cooperate with colleagues (N=120)	34.2	40	9.2	8.3	8.3	100
Inefficient—Efficient (N=120)	27.5	26.7	34.2	5.8	5.8	100
Unconcerned—Concerned with inmates (N=120)	5.8	5.8	40.8	14.2	34.2	100
Lazy—Hard-working (N=120)	41.7	30	19.2	0.8	8.3	100
Strict—Considerate (N=120)	60	20	10.8	8.3	0.8	100
Ignorant—Knowledgeable (N=120)	2.5	4.2	23.3	28.3	41.7	100
Corrupt—Honest (N=120)	31.7	19.2	39.2	6.7	3.3	100
Shaky—Bold (N=120)	2.5	5.8	25.8	15.8	50.0	100

not cooperate with colleagues. Next, he is corrupt man as also inefficient in his work. But, interestingly enough, he is bold and a knowledgeable fellow. These last mentioned traits namely bold knowledgeability should attract attention. The possibility cannot be ruled out that misfit but bold and knowledgeable officers create many problems for others.

Staff Optimism : If a positive and optimistic approach is important for the inmates; it is equally important for the officials. There may be a plethora of problems : unsatisfactory emoluments, slow advancement in the career, idiosyncracies of the superiors, and so forth. However, the officials in their respective ranks and positions have not only to maintain composure but also be hopeful about the future. It is easy to suggest that the pessimists would seldom be able to put in requisite attention or energy in their work. In this regard, the position of the officials in the present sample may be ascertained. They were given a hypothetical situation and their responses have been ascertained (Table 4.16) Refreshingly enough, majority of the staff members (90.8%) feel that a better future

TABLE 4.16

Responses of the officials to the question, "Do you think that certain recent changes in the government policy concerning jail working promise better future for jail employees ?

	No	Can't say	Yes	Total
Frequency	02	09	109	120
Percentage	1.7	7.5	90.8	100

awaits jail employees. What is more noteworthy, is that their education is somewhat related to this ($p < 0.0244$). It is supported by the length of service of the staff members ($p < .0034$). This is to say that more than three-fourths of the staff members who have been serving in jail department for more than a decade, are hopeful about a better future.

Job Satisfaction : It may be reiterated that the jail working demands more than regulatory functioning. Ideally speaking, jail functionaries whether performing custodial, administrative or treatment functions are called upon to have a missionary zeal, commitment and dedication. A correctional institution would be able to realise its objectives to the extent the, correspondingly, functionaries manning it are motivated. This is not to say that the onus of realising institutional objectives is wholly and solely on the functionaries. Directly or indirectly, the organisation has an equally important role. The organisational policy, resources, procedures and the like are important. Equally, if not more important, are personnel policies. That men who have the aptitude, who enjoy human relations and who are willing to help others are brought in, is directly dependent on the recruitment policy. Similarly, their sustained interest and involvement in the institutional work would depend mainly on the training programmes they are exposed to, opportunities of career advancement they are provided, the salary and perquisites they are offered and, above all, on the organisational ethos. It is, thus, obvious that the concept of job satisfaction would seldom be more relevant anywhere else than in the context of correctional institutions.

It has already been mentioned that only the Superintendent, a Deputy Superintendent alongwith one Senior Jailor may be regarded as having a supervisory status. Among the remaining officials about 20% occupy intermediate rungs, and the rest, subordinate status. This may have implications for job satisfaction. Besides, most important among the perquisites, is the provision of government quarters. Jail employees, like other state employees are entitled to government accommodation or failing which to house rent allowance (HRA). However, the HRA is hardly adequate to rent entitled accommodation. This is what makes the provisions of government quarters a perquisite. However, it is gratifying to note that 90 per cent of the staff members live in the government residential quarters, only 10% of the jail staff of the jail under study do not have government quarters.

With this in view, an attempt may be made to look into a

few other dimensions which may have a bearing on the level of job-satisfaction of the officials.

Promotions : In any scheme of incentives to the functionaries, promotions would rank among the foremost. In the absence of adequate promotion openings, they may stagnate and thereby lose interest in their work. Were they to continue with the job owing to precarious employment situation in the region or country, they would be in the main current. Equally frustrating would be the position if promotions do not follow on open and judicious policy. Earlier, a mention has been made regarding limited growth opportunities in the jail service. Besides, whatever promotions are granted, they are initially on *adhoc* basis and thereby leave many promotees uncertain and insecure. The position may now be examined in relation to the present sample.

A perusal of Table 4.17 would show that an overwhelming majority (67.5%) of the officials had not received no promotions ad hoc or otherwise. To be specific, only six officials have received two or more promotions. This connect up with the observation made earlier : jail service has extremely limited

TABLE 4.17

Number of Promotions of Staff Members

	None	One	Two	Three	Total
Frequency	81	33	04	02	120
Percentage	67.5	27.3	3.3	1.7	100

promotion avenues. This aside, it is hardly surprising that factors like length of service, functional status and prior experience of the officials are highly related to the number of promotions they have received ($p < .0001$). In other words, whatever limited advancement opportunities are available, they go by seniority. This is what is further supported by the analysis which follows. An attempt has been made to ascertain the opinion of the officials, about the basis of promotion in the jail department. On going through the Table 4.18, it would be noticed that positive considerations, like seniority, good conduct, hard work and superior opinion have been emphasised in this regard. Nonetheless, certain negative considerations, like flattery of superiors and support from the influential have also been underlined. Focusing on positive aspects, seniority

TABLE 4.18

Response of the official to the question, "In your opinion what are the two important basis for promotion in your department ?

	I preference		II preference		Weightet prefe-rence
	Frequeney	Percentage	Frequency	Percentage	
Seniority	65	54.6	39	33.9	46.9
Good conduct	49	41.2	42	36.5	38.8
Competence	01	0.8	05	4.2	1.9
Support from the influentials	02	1.7	12	10.4	4.4
Money power	—	—	01	0.8	.2
Superior opinion	01	0.8	09	7.8	3.05
Educational status	—	—	04	3.5	1.1
Hard work	02	1.7	08	7.0	3.3
Total	120	100	120	100	100

clearly a high weights every other considerations. While seniority maintains objectivity in the promotion process, an overemphasis on it may engender indifference or even stoicism among the officials. This aside, the present data may be examined along with those presented in Table 4.17. It is difficult to escape the impression that promotions in the jail service are few and far between. It hardly matters that promotions are granted purely on merit or not if openings for career advancement are so very limited.

That limited promotion chances generate disaffection and frustrations is easy to suggest. The frustration would further deepen should the level of aspiration among the officials be high. This is what is sought to be ascertained through the data presented in Table 4.19. The opinion of the officials has been elicited whether they could handle the job of their immediate superior. More than ninetyfour per cent of them state that

TABLE 4.19

Response of the officials to the question, "In case you promoted could you do the job of your immediate superior ?"

	Easily	With some training	After some experience	Not sure	Total
Frequency	113	03	03	01	120
Percentage	94.2	2.5	2.5	0.8	100

they could easily; and only nearly six per cent of them express reservations. Apparently, a vast majority of the officials is ambitious and may have been eagerly looking forward to a promotion for long. This contention is further reinforced when the data are examined in relation to the length of service of the official ($p<.0666$). The officials who have put in large number of years find themselves capable of handling easily the job of their immediate superior. Perhaps promotion prospects in the jails call for a review.

Liking for the job : Needless to state that in a goal-oriented organisation like jail it is extremely important that functionaries identified themselves with their organisation and job. Contrariwise, should their job approximate to their perferences, they and hence their organisation would be able to achieve desired results. In this connection, the opinion of the officials may be examined (see Table 4.20). It would not take long to see that majority (61.7%) of the staff members like the nature of work in the jail in some respects, while 28.3% of them like their job much. On the other hand, only 5% of them do not like their job in jail. This suggest satisfaction on the part of officials with their work. This dimension shows significant variations with personal or professional characteristics of the officials for example, education of the staff numbers ($p < .0131$); functional branch ($p < .0001$) and the length of the service of the officials ($p < .0513$).

TABLE 4.20

Responses of the officials to the question, "Do you like the nature of your present work in the jail ?"

	Not at all	In some respect	Much	Very much	Can't say	Total
Frequency	06	74	34	04	02	120
Percentage	0.5	61.7	28.3	3.3	1.7	100

The above mentioned theme has been persued further. The view of the officials has been ascertained with regard to certain features like security of service, prestige in society and so forth (Table 4.21). The most outstanding features of the jail service, as rated by the officials, are the security of service, appreciation by the superiors, co-operation from colleagues, easy nature of work, and the prestige in society. It may be noted that chance to help or popularity among inmates rank only sixth and seventh. It is, however, gratifying to note that only vocational or treatment staff give importance to these in their work. This apart, the low priority accorded to the remunerative aspects of the jail service should not escape the attention. These aspects would be further analysed a little later.

Attractive features of the job : The perception of the job, and its attractive or unattractive features are likely to provide a dependable estimate of the level of job-satisfaction among the officials. Furthermore, this may also indicate as to what extent the officials are career-oriented or service-oriented. Towards this, to begin with the most attractive feature of the job as

TABLE 4.21

Response of the officials to the question, "Relating to their present job in the jail which of the features mentioned below are applicable ?" (Percentage)

	Appli-cable	Uncer-tain	Not applicable	Total
Security of service	100	—	—	100
Appreciation by superiors	89.2	0.8	10	100
Popularity among inmates	6.7	1.7	91.7	100
Cooperation from colleagues	40.8	2.5	56.7	100
Good income	1.7	0.8	97.5	100
Chance to help inmates	18.3	—	81.7	100
Prestige in society	25.8	—	74.2	100
Easy nature of work	27.5	0.8	70.7	100

perceived by the officials may be looked into (see Table 4.22). It would be readily seen that first three preferences are for what

TABLE 4.22

Response of the officials to the question, "Relating to your present job in the jail. What are the two most attractive features ?"

	I Preference		II Preference		Weightet prefe-rence
	Frequency	%	Frequency	%	
Security of service	115	95.8	02	1.7	64.4
Prestige in society	—	—	07	5.8	1.9
Cooperation from colleagues	—	—	04	3.3	1.1
Chance to help inmates	04	3.3	03	2.5	3.05
Appreciation by superiors	01	0.8	98	81.7	27.7
Easy work	—	—	03	2.5	0.8
Popularity among inmates	—	—	03	2.5	0.8
Total	120	100	120	100	100

may be termed as career-oriented features. To be explicit, security of service is emphasised. On the other hand, service oriented features like chance to help inmates and popularity among inmates occupy third and sixth place respectively in rank order. Like all government organisations, the jail department offers security of service which appeals most to the officials in view of the surfeit in the labour market.

What are the unattractive features ? The data presented in Tables 4.21 and 4.22 suggest that salary, working with criminals and so on are not much to the liking of the officials. In addition, an attempt has been made to ascertain the least attractive features of the job as perceived by the officials (see Table 4.23). It would be seen that the career aspects such as salary, promotion and working conditions mostly are least attractive features as reported by the officials. Next to these, dealing with criminals by the staff comes up with nominal weightet preference of 3.3. Apparently, the officials are given to dealing with inmates in a more or less a mechanical manner. Notwithstanding this, the relative inadequacy of the incentives offered to the officials

TABLE 4.23

Responses of the officials to the question, "What are the two least attractive features of your present job ?"

	I Preference		II Preference		Weightet preference
	Frequency	%	Frequency	%	
Salary	114	95	04	3.3	64.4
Promotions	05	4.2	74	61.7	23.3
Working conditions	—	—	31	25.8	8.6
Harsh superiors	—	—	01	0.8	0.2
Dealing with criminals	01	0.8	10	8.3	3.3
Total	120	100	120	100	100

including salary and promotions discussed earlier. It is further underscored by the information presented here.

Job perception : The above line of analysis has been pursued further. Using semi-projective statements, an attempt has been made to explore the way the officials look at their job (see Table 4.24). A glance on the distribution of the data would show that in respect of few statements the response of the officials is positive : more than thirty per cent of the staff members feel that they are doing something useful in their job. A vast majority of the officials (80%) feel that their present job provides them lot of pleasure and is not be boring at all for them. On the other hand, in relation to the statement, "If I get....", and "I would like my son....", the opinion of the officials is clearly negative. In respect of these two mentioned statements, in fact, a larger numbers (71.7% and 95% respecti-

TABLE 4.24

Response of the officials to the question, "Do you agree or disagree with the following statements about your job?" (Percentages)

Statement	Disagree	Can't say	Agree	Total
This work give me a lot of pleasure	17.5	2.5	80	100
For me this job is boring	80.8	1.7	17.5	100
I am doing something useful in the job	11.7	56.7	30.7	100
If I get government equivalent job equally paying, I would leave the present one.	27.5	0.8	71.7	100
I would like my son also to join jail service.	95.0	0.8	4.2	100

vely) of the officials have shown strong disinclination about leaving of the present job on getting another equivalent job and joining of jail service by their sons.

Interestingly enough, functional branch of the officials appears to influence their job perception of the officials. Vocational staff has a more positive view of its job than those belonging to custodial staff. In order to secure a comprehensive view of job perception, the responses presented in Table 4.24 have been indexed, the scores have been trichotomised and the distribution is presented in Table 4.25. It would be seen

TABLE 4.25

Job perception by the officials

	Low	Medium	High	Total
Frequency	20	70	30	120
Percentage	16.7	58.3	25.0	100

from the data that more than half (58.3%) of staff members may be regarded as having average job perception and one-fourth of the officials having high job perception. Taken together, it has to asserted that jail service is held high esteem by the officials themselves.

Role Identification : Jails have seldom been easy places to manage. They have a normative structure which is characterised by inmate and staff culture and ethos governing staff-inmate relationship (Holt, 1977). Stated differentially, the officials who are in constant contact with the inmates are "the most important figures in the institution and in fact in the entire system" (Verin, 1973). The realisation of the correctional objectives would directly hinge on their capacity and the degree to which they are able to identify their role.

The significance of the role of the watch and ward staff may be underlined. Indeed, their role is mainly custodial but day in and day out they interact with inmates. Divested from a correctional approach and concerned solely with custodial duties, their working cannot but cause tensions (Grutzner, 1971). Their role and activities, therefore, have to have a correctional approach (Brown, et al., 1971; Sepe and Trucco, 1973). What has been the position in the present context ? To answer this question satisfactorily, role identification, role norms and role adherence among the officials may be examined. Further, the extent and quality of staff-inmate interaction may also be ascertained.

Role Perception : The institutional correction, it is generally agreed, has to go beyond incarceration. The inmate has to be exposed to a programme which would help him in changing his ideas, behaviour and skills so as to get reintegrated into society after release. Implicit in all this is that jail officials particularly those at the cutting-edge level identify themselves with the task they are supposed to accomplish. Much of it, of course, would

TABLE 4.26

Response to the officials to the question, "Do you agree or disagree with the following statements ?"

(Percentage)

Statement	Disagree	Can't say	Agree	Total
In jail working it would not matter if one person does not work.	10.8	9.2	80	100
The work in the jail allows officials to use their capabilities	2.5	8.3	89.2	100
No matter what amount of effort you make but the quality of work in your branch in the jail is not going to improve much.	25.8	53.3	20.8	100

depend upon how they perceive themselves in their organisational framework (Peretti and Hooker, 1976). This is what has been assessed in the present context (see Table 4.26). It would be noticed that more than three-fourths of the officials feel that it would not affect jail working if one person does not work; is far from encouraging. The level of bureaucratisation has perhaps taken a heavy toll as far as the initiative of individual functionaries is concerned. Refreshingly enough, functional branch of the officials is closely linked with this aspect of role identification of the staff members (tau= -0.24354; $p<.0001$). It is also supported by functional status of the officials with this ($p<.0051$).

That bureaucratic working has instilled much inertia is further supported by the response pattern with regard to the statement, "the work in the jail allows........", the majority (89.2%) of the officials show agreement with this. Although the working in the jail has become much routinised and procedure bound. Even then they (officials) have got opportunity to show their capability in their job.

The officials, nevertheless, are somewhat oblivious of the significance of initiative and drive of individual functionaries. About more than one-fourth of the officials feel that quality of work in their branch could improve much with the added effort on the part of functionaries.

Using the response-pattern reflected in Table 4.26 a composite variable has been developed (see Table 4.27). This may

TABLE 4.27

Role perception of the officials

	Low	Medium	High	Total
Frequency	33	75	12	120
Percentage	27.5	62.5	10	100

facilitate in securing a comprehensive view of the professional esteem of the officials. That bulk (62.5%) of officials have an average level of role perception is hardly unexpected. What is, however, noteworthy is the fact that more than one-fourth of officials having low role perception is larger than those having a high role of perception (10%). The relatively low level of role perception may have adverse implications for correctional programmes particularly work programmes in the jail.

Role Norm : To what extent jails have been able to bring about a change in their approach to crime and the crime-doer, is best reflected in the role norms of the functionaries (Peretti and Hooker, 1976). However, the process of ascertaining role norms is difficult to operationalise. Being value-loaded, the

TABLE 4.28

Perception of the role norms among the officials? (Percentage)

Items	Not important	Can't say	Important	Total
Is it important to you to work hard without bothering about reward or promotions ? (N=120)	0.8	0.8	98.3	100
Is it important to you to keep inmates satisfied and happy ? (N=120)	—	—	100	100
Is it important to you to help and guide inmates to improve their conduct and ideas ? (N=120)	—	0.8	99.2	100
Is it important to you to control inmates so as to ensure security in jail ? (N=120)	—	—	100	100

items designed to bring out role norms tend to bring out affirmative responses. This is what would be readily seen on going through the data presented in Table 4.28. A vast majority of the officials have a clear understanding of their role norms. An overwhelming majority feels that they should work selflessly keep inmate satisfied and happy and help them to improve their conduct. Yet another fact which would attract attention is the emphasis on jail security : almost all of them find it important to control inmates so as to ensure security. This kind of emphasis or over-emphasis on the security aspect may overshadow correctional programmes.

It may not be out of place to have an integrated view of the role norms as perceived by the officials (see Table 4.29). It would be seen that all of the officials have high level of perception of their role norm, falls into the expected pattern.

The data presented in tables 4.28 and 4.29 represent the opinion of the officials as to what they ought to do. To what extent they are able to translate these ideatory positions into their functioning can be assessed from those whom they serve and interact with. A reference to Table 2.16 would show that a vast majority of the inmates feel that the jail authorities are impartial in the assignment of job and trades to them. That

TABLE 4.29
Perception of role norms.

	Low	Medium	High	Total
Frequency	—	—	120	120
Percentage	—	—	100	100

vocational instructors are by and large helpful in teaching them trades is brought out by the data presented in Table 4.30. However, the fact may not be lost sight of that vocational instructors may be a shade different from custodial staff in their dealing with the inmates.

TABLE 4.30

Response of the inmates to the question, "Do you find your present instructors helpful in teaching you trades?"

	Not helpful	Indifferent	Helpful	Total
Frequency	15	38	284	337
Percentage	4.5	11.3	84.3	100

Role adherence: Helping inmates to change their ideas and conduct is an uphill task. They must be stimulated to activity, inventiveness, thought and reflection. On the whole, the task makes heavy demands on the jail officials including custodial staff and vocational instructors (Montagano, 1971). Earlier, role norms among the officials have been ascertained; now an attempt may be made to ascertain the extent to which the officials adhere to these roles (see table 4.31). The three statements designed to bring out role adherence by the officials are to a good deal affirmed by the officials. Apparently, a sizable proportion of the officials do or try to help the inmates. Beside this majority (89.2%) of the officials try to keep them satisfied and happy. In assessment of the officials themselves, there is a very small (2.5%) section of the officials which does not altogether feel concerned with these imperatives. For the second or next aspect, majority (84.2%) of the official feel that they help and guide inmates for improving their conduct and ideas. This aside, the security aspect (characterised by repeated headcounts, punctilious lockup and watch towers) is underlined once again. About 90.8% of the official state that most of them control inmates so as to ensure security in the jail. This kind of obsession with security may satisfy the requirements of role adherence, but may fall short of the institutional objectives of reformation and rehabilitation. This is not to suggest that jails should be unmindful of security. Security and security arrangements must be there but they may well not become an end into themselves.

TABLE 4.31

Role adherence among the officials (Percentages).

Statements	None of them	Some of them	Most of them	Total
Do you think jail officials keep inmates satisfied and happy? (N=120)	2.5	8.3	89.2	100
Do you think jail officials help and guide inmates to improve their conduct and ideas? (N=120)	—	15.8	84.2	100
Do you think jail officials control inmates so as to ensure security in jail? (N=120)	0.8	8.3	90.8	100

TABLE 4.32

Role adherence among the jail officials.

	Low	Medium	High	Total
Frequency	—	01	119	120
Percentage	—	0.8	99.2	100

The response pattern shown in Table 4.31 has been indexed and a composite variable has been generated. The distribution is present in Table 4.32. In the self-assessment of the officials the level of role adherence among them is high, indeed. For obvious reasons, this assessment may not be free from bias. An assessment by those whom they serve namely inmates, may be a little more meaningful.

TABLE 4.33

Inmate assessment of role adherence by the staff (Percentage).

Statement	None of them	Some of them	Most of them	Total
Do you think that the officials work hard without bothering about reward or promotion? (N=337)	30	32.9	37.1	100
Do you think that jail officials keep inmates satisfied and happy? (N=337)	17.2	27.3	55.5	100
Do you think that jail officials help and guide inmates to improve their conduct and ideas? (N=337)	22	22	56.1	100
Do you think jail officials control inmates so as to ensure security in the jail? (N=337)	4.2	10.4	85.5	100

A reference to Table 4.33 brings out the view of the inmates on the extent of role adherence among the officials. In the opinion of only 37.1% of the inmates most of the officials are given to selfless working. In contrast, 30% of them are categorical that none of the officials is unconcerned with reward or promotion. Are they careerists? In respect of officials keeping inmates satisfied and happy, the view of the inmates appears to be better than that of the officials themselves (see Table 4.31). More than half of the inmates, feel that most of the officials work towards their satisfaction and happiness. So is not the case with regard to officials being helpful in the reformation of the inmates (Table 4.33). The inmates' 'opinion seems at best divided. The security aspect in the jail is further confirmed by the inmates' opinion. About 85.5% of them feel that most of the officials control inmates for security reasons. It would not be surprising if an equal proportion of the inmates is found endorsing security arrangement—so pervasive may be the influence of disculturation in the jail.

Staff-inmate interaction : The therapautic value of the staff-inmate interaction in an institutional setting can hardly be overestimated. A smooth, intense and professional relationship with the inmates would enable the staff to empathise and to get into their innerself. This is likely to go in securing an insight into the capacity as well as thc limitation of the inmates and hence in individualising on them of the correctional impact.

However, it needs to be pointed out that staff-inmate interaction by itself may not be in conformity with the institutional objectives. Certain amout of inane interaction between staff and inmate has been noticed during the data collection. The officials, particularly those in the lower rung, may be friendly with the rowdy inmates or may connive at the high-handed dealings of the convict officers. Such interaction serves little purpose; on the contrary, it may have a negative value. Likewise, there is what could be termed as motivated interaction. The officials may have been approached by the friends, relatives or the inmate himself. They may deal with him in a much considerate way. Notwithstanding these abnormal interactional situations. What is and should be emphasised is the professional interaction based on an understanding of human nature and a willingness to help the needy. Such interaction is likely to impart the requisite therapeutic influence.

Keeping the above in view the nature of staff-inmate interaction may be examined. Earlier (Table 2.13) an estimate has been provided as to how much time the officials spend in contact or conversation with the inmates. It is found that 64.2% of them spend most of their working time in such interaction. It is realised that the nature of duties involving contact with the inmate differs from position to position. Officials, like Warder or Assistant Jailors, may have to be in touch with the residents most of the time, while the Jailor or Jail Superintendent,

TABLE 4.34

Response of the officials to the question, "Do you personally enjoy contacts or conversation with the inmates?"

	Not at all	Have to tolerate	A little	Very much	Total
Frequency	14	60	39	07	120
Percentage	11.7	50	32.5	5.8	100

Deputy Jail Superintendent, only occasionally do so. What is, therefore, important is the individual view of such contact or interaction. On going through Table 4.34, it would be seen that only 5.8% of the officials enjoy such interaction; as against this, 11.7% of them do not at all like this. Apparently, traditional notions about crime and crime-doers continue inhibiting smooth staff-inmate interaction. More relevant is also the consideration as to how much correctional influence the staff is able to impart in view of this kind of inhibited interaction.

On this, the view point of the inmates may also be brought in. To a good deal, staff-inmate interaction has to be problem-solving what is the opinion of the inmates in this regard? A perusal of Table 4.35 would readily show that 73.6% of the inmates agree that the jail authorities try to solve their problems rather than find faults with them. The fact, however, should

TABLE 4.35

Response of the inmates to the statement, "Jail authorities try to solve the problem of the inmates rather than find faults with them."

	Disagree	Can't say	Agree	Total
Frequency	75	14	248	337
Percentage	22.3	4.2	73.6	100

not be lost sight of that nearly 22.3% of them show disagreement in this regard. In a service organisation, this kind of negative feelings on the part of the clientele hardly speak well. Also, it is difficult to escape the impression that the curative potential of staff-inmate interaction in jail is yet to be fully exploited.

The quality of manpower resources and the organisational ethos are important in any organisation but they are crucial to institutional correction. This is what has been explored in the present section. It is found that a typical jail official is male, a Hindu and Brahmin by caste. Middle aged and married, he has done schooling above VIII standard. He has little by way of pre-entry or on job training although he has been in jail service for about 15 years. As a subordinate official, he is engaged in custodial duties. He may discuss his professional problems with colleagues but seldom with superiors.

Having received no promotion and his ambiting being fairly high, he particularly does not like his job; and there are several real and imaginary reasons for this. He does have any idea as to what he is supposed to do, yet he may not be always able to translate his ideas into practice.

Keeping this in view, it is difficult to conclude that the officials in the jail under study are sufficiently oriented in reformatory ideals. The fact that only about 19% of their discount 'chance to help inmate' and only 7% of them discount 'popularity among inmates' as job-features is hardly encouraging. Evidence is recurrent that custodial orientation overrides everything else including reformatory ideals. What is more, nearly half of them are averse to dealing with inmates. In fact, the analysis shows that inevitability of dealing with inmates inherent to their job weighs heavy on their level of job-satisfaction. The hypothesis is, thus, not substantiated by the data.

5

The Work-Programmes

Indeed, many perceptive accounts are available, which deal with treatment programme in jails. For example, Banks (1958) and Roberts (1969) have focalised the programme of general education provided to jail-inmates. A superabundance is, however, noticed with respect to work programmes. The work release programme, which is old and new, has been studied by many researchers (see Case, 1967; Grupp and Verin, 1968; Johnson, 1970). Different vocational trades from carpentry to electronic data processing have been brought under focus (Vanbuskirk, 1964; Gordon, 1967; Sellin, 1967; Caird, 1972; Hodgkin, 1972; Wenk and Frank, 1973). Relating to the Indian scene, a few descriptive accounts are available dealing with treatment programmes in general (see, for example, Khan, 1976; Trivedi, 1978; Srivastava, 1977; and Singh, 1979). Concerning work programmes, some empirical data have also been collected (see Khan and Unnithan, 1978; Unnithan and Khan, 1978 and 1979). Thus, it would not take long to see that, in the Indian Social context, little concerted effort has been made to look into policy objectives and the organisation of treatment programmes, in general, and work programmes, in particular, or to ascertain the level of interest of and participation by the inmates in these programmes.

To state the obvious, there is a qualitative difference between having a range of treatment programmes in our institution and realising the intrinsic objectives underlying them. This gap or gulf is obvious in respect of work programmes which, through time and space, have variously signified penal servitude, raw exploitation of captive labour or an important therapeutic means. It is, therefore, more than a desirability, to enquire into the nature, organisation and working of work programmes. This is what has been attempted in the present section. Towards this end, it proceeds to examine a descriptive hypothesis: *In their organisation and working, the work programmes in the institutions are purposive and inmate-oriented.*

It may be reiterated here that the term "treatment programmes" includes within its scope: (1) employment upon essential jail services as well as outside the jail and remunerative work both inside and outside the jail; (2) academic education; (3) vocational training; (4) recreation, sports, atheletics and related informal activities; (5) religious services and counselling; (6) formal group counselling and social case work; and (7) training in self-reliance and self-government (see also, Hooper, 1964). For the present purposes, only vocational training and employment of the inmates are the substantive concern.

Yet another point to be clarified relates to the employment of inmates. There are in use several systems to put inmates to work; lease, contract, accord, public works, state use and public control (for details, see Murton, 1976). In the institution under study, the inmates were deployed for 'state use' or for inmate-service, and for jail maintenance work. All these uses of inmate-labour have been, for the present purposes, grouped under the term work programmes. This is not without justification. Every kind of training and experience, whenever and however gained, which is designed and calculated to equip the inmate with skill and knowledge to obtain and retain honest employment and become self-supporting on his return to society, has been aptly regarded by the Canadian Penitentiary Service as vocational training (see also, Baril, 1967).

Thus, in order to examine the hypothesis laid down earlier, the nature of work programmes in the institution, the purpose underlying them as perceived by the parties concerned, the extent to which these programmes match the background and needs of the inmates, the infrastructure available for work programmes, motivations offered to inmates, and allied issues have been looked into.

NATURE OF WORK

Indeed, the potential and the promise of work programmes in the reformation, reclamation and rehabilitation of jail inmates is enormous. Much, however, depends on a forwardlooking institutional policy, imaginative planning of the work programmes and their implementation in spirit as well as in latter. As mentioned earlier, in order to realise the enunciated objectives, the range of available work programmes ought to approximate to the psycho-social needs of the inmates and serve to equip them for a smooth readjustment in the community after release.

Generally speaking, the correctional institutions in the country have three work units, at times overlapping, in which they put the labour of inmates to use : (i) vocational training and production, (ii) inmates services, and (iii) maintenance work. Besides this, some select inmates are elevated to the position of convict officers (see Chapter Two). These convict officers work in factorysheds, hospital and jail office and oversee the work of other inmates. In assigning work to inmates, most institutions are often faced with the problem of making a policy decision—whether to be led by *the manpower requirements* of the work units, or to be guided by the *individual needs* of the inmates. A similar policy dilemma appears to beset the appointment of convict officers. As the appointment of convict officers has been dealt with earlier, for the present attention may be focused on vocational trades, inmate services and maintenance unit.

For several reasons, work programmes in the jails in the country have become considerably diversified. Inmates have been put on mechanised farming and systematic dairyfarming. Some institutions have introduced modern trades like letter-printing, soap making, paper-making and brasswaremaking. In certain jails, the inmates are trained to repair tractors and other agro-equipments. In the jail under study, the range of available trades appears to be at somewhat limited (see Table 5.01) :

TABLE 5.01
Work assigned to the inmates in the Model Prison, Lucknow

Vocational trades	Number of inmates
Agriculture	39
Spinning and Gauze-bandage	33
Weaving	35
Powerloom and Dyeing	37
Tailoring	16
Paper-making	13
Oil-press mechine	15
Baan Kaman	04
Inmate Service :	
Kitchen/cooking	24
Clerical work	03
Godown/store	11
Other service—Barber, Laundry, Mulahja	08
Maintenance Unit :	
Sweeping/cleaning	29
Raj Kaman	08
Gardening	26
Convict Officers :	
Night watchman	09
Overseers	21
Warders	06
Total	337

agriculture, weaving, powerloom, tailoring, handmade paper-making and oil-press machine. This apart, inmate services are also there including clerical work, clothing, kitchen and miscellaneous work. As in the case of most jails, much emphasis is laid on maintenance work involving sweeping, cleaning and Raj Kaman. It would not be out of place to provide a few more details of some prominent units (for details see, Trivedi, 1984).

Agriculture Unit : In keeping with the predominantly rural character of the inmate population, agriculture has received sufficient priority in the jail. Besides the jail building; some land is available (about 60 acres) which is used for farming and 'vegiculture'. About 30 inmates regularly work on the land, and during the sowing and harvesting seasons, a few more hands are put on the job. There is no instructor, and inmates under the supervision of head warders go about farming using the experience they themselves possess.

A few years ago, the land bullocks and old-styled ploughs were used for the cultivation of land. Mainly dependent on monsoons, dug-wells provided meagre irrigation facilities. However, sometime ago, the Government of Uttar Pradesh ammended the Uttar Pradesh Sahkarita Adhinium, 1965, so that convicts may officially form a co-operative society. For this, the Jail Department prepared a plan in collaboration with the State Bank of India, under which on 22nd Nov., 1975, a Model Prison Seva Sahkaree Samitee Limited has been registered, which consists of 50 inmate members. There is another management committee which is working under the above said cooperative society which includes 15 convicts of the institution and the Superintendent, as its Chairman. These measures have been very fruitful in improving the position of the agriculture section and the other work sheds of the institution, and to develop a sense of self-independence among the inmates, by providing modern facilities and equipments. This way, the agriculture section, meant for those inmates who live in huts freely outside the jail at agricultural farm the day and night, known as 'Bihari Kaidi' has become self-reliant. From this section, some of the convicts also go for daily-wages work in government gardens and Sugarcane Research Institute. Recently, the cooperative society of the institution has purchased a tractor worth Rs. 49,000/-. In addition to this, the society has installed a tube-well by taking a loan from the State Bank of India of Rs. 20,000/-, and Rs. 3,308/- for the purchase of mechanical cultivators. This aside, 15 inmates of this section has taken loans totalling Rs. 45,000/- from the bank for the purchase of buffalo to organise a dairy farm.

Powerloom Unit : In the left portion of the jail enclosure, there is 'Ganga Bhawan', meant for '*Adarshi Kaidies*' (ideal inmates). A big mechanised powerloom work-shed, is located on the left side of the gate of this 'Bhawan'. The section consists of a large room (about 12×6 metres), with an attached store-room at the opposite side of the unit. In the large room, 2 mechanised powerlooms are installed. The unit has the position of two trained instructors. They supervise the work in the unit. In this section about thirtyseven inmates work and learn, and systematic efforts are made to impart instructions. Using cotton yarn, it produces single and double threaded table cloths, sarees for the female inmates of Nari Bandi Grah, Lucknow, and General cloth for the dress of the inmates. In 1976, this unit produced goods worth Rs. 84,676/-.

Hand-made Paper Making : Adjacent to the powerloom unit, is the hand-made paper making unit. As a matter of fact, it is physically somewhat similar to the powerloom unit—the major differences are that this unit is not so mechanised and it provides work to a much smaller number of inmates i.e., only 13 who are supervised by a trained instructor. This unit is very peculiar in the institution, under study, at least among the U.P. Jails. This unit produces many different type of paper. In 1976, the value of the paper produced in this unit, was Rs. 15,327. It may be added that this section is only meant for '*Adarsh Kaidies*' (ideal inmates) of the 'Ganga Bhawan' as in the case of former work unit (power-loom).

Weaving Unit : This work unit is situated in the right portion of the jail enclosure in the 'Jamuna Bhawan'. The entire section consists of Durri and Niwar making sub-sections.

The physical set-up of this unit is somewhat similar to those described earlier. Along the length of the room is located the loom and the warping bay. On the other side of the room, on one corner has a spindle-wheel and other small equipments. Under the supervision of a trained instructor, about thirtyfive inmates work here, on an average day. Needed raw material included yarn and dye are usually brought from Kanpur. Niwar, towels, bedsheets, durri, carpet, and coarse cloths are the main product. In the range of its produce, durries are much in demand particularly by the Government Offices. A substantial portion of the niwar produced in the unit goes, through commercial channels, to open market through the Jail Depot, Lucknow, while other items are mostly sold to government departments, including the Jail Department through the Jail Depot.

Kitchen : In the range of inmate-services, the most notable, and perhaps the most arduous, is the work in the jail kitchen. In the square shaped, high ceilinged and tile-thatched, smallish room, food is cooked to serve three meals a day to some four hundred residents. The kitchen uses firewood in open hearths, large aluminium pots, for preparing gravy, and large *tawas* (outsized iron-plates), for baking *chapattis*, cereals, vegetables, if needed, condiments, fire-wood and miscellaneous items for the kitchen are arranged for by the Superintendent of the jail and supplied by a local contractor.

Despite ventilators, the kitchen remains almost throughout the day filled with smoke, vapour and heat. While four or five inmates operate the electrically run flour mill, about 24 inmates, every day, handle various kitchen chores. Most trying is the work of those who bake *chapattis.* Even during summer, when the mercury touches about 460C, they have to brave the heat often for six hours a day. It may be added that not only are uppercaste Hindus preferred for the kitchen work, but also that kitchen hands are seldom rotated to other work or trades.

A reference to Table 5.01 would readily show that the inmates are put to work in several other ways, as well. The inmates who are relatively better educated are assigned to the jail office or stores to share clerical work. Quite a large number of inmates are assigned work in accordance with their caste. To illustrate the point, *dhobi* inmates are ready candidates for the inmate-laundry (although meant for residents, it also launders the clothing of the jail staff). The inmates who are *nai* (barber) by caste, undertake the haircutting of other inmates. As a matter of fact, this service is rendered exclusively by barber-inmates. Interesting is the case of the cleaning-sweeping unit. While inmates belonging to the scavenger caste are usually assigned to this unit, others are also sent to it, at least in their early days in the jail.

Inmate Distribution : In order to get at the priority accorded by the institution to various work units and trades, the distribution of the inmates may now be focalised. Among work units, there are assigned to vocational trades about 64% of the inmates. However, other units have an equally substantial number of inmates, inmate services (15%), maintenance unit (21%), Convict officers (11%). If we turn our attention to vocational trades (N=192), the maximum number of inmates assigned is to the agriculture, (20.3%), powerloom and dyeing, (19.3%), weaving (18.2%) and spinning (17.2%). In the category inmate services (N=46), the bulk of the inmates (52%) are engaged in the kitchen.

Are the work avenues offered to the inmates in the jail purposive and inmate-oriented ? It may be emphasised that the work or trade which is aligned to the occupational pattern or manpower needs of the outside community, has a greater likelihood of helping the inmates in their economic rehabilitation after release. Does the work assigned to the inmates measure up to this? Inmate services and maintenance work may be helpful in instilling useful work-habits in the inmates; yet it would be difficult to presume that they would facilitate post-release rehabilitation. This apart, the work in such units like kitchen and cleaning-sweeping unit may cause aversion towards the institutional correction and resentment towards work.

Focusing on vocational trades, agriculture, including farming and gardening, has much relevance. Since the majority of the inmates are from rural areas, agriculture as a trade is particularly useful. Indeed, it has received the priority as it deserves. The number of inmates assigned to agriculture is sufficient (N=39); it has no instructor and the agricultural practices are somewhat traditional. Consequently, inmates have only a remote chance of picking up a skill which they already do not have. The trade powerloom, weaving, spinning and tailoring are doubtless aligned to the needs of the community outside. To a great extent, skills in weaving, spinning, powerloom and dyeing and papermaking may come in handy to many an inmate after release. The need for giving weaving a rural bias may be, however, emphasised. Trained in any of these, an inmate could seldom hope to start his own business : the supply of raw material, capital investment and the distribution of the finished product would be quite a problem to him. Nor could he easily get a salaried job. Apparently, the policy relating to utilisation of labour of the inmates, the range of work programmes in the jail and the pattern of vocational trades offered to the inmates call for a thorough review.

PURPOSE BEHIND WORK

It is generally agreed that institutional correction has four broad policy objectives : (a) restraint of the convicted offenders, (b) their reformation, (c) their rehabilitation after release, and (d) their reintegration into society (see also Duffee, 1975). Restraint or curtailment of liberty is implicit in institutionalisation and the remaining three objectives are sought to be realised through different correctional programmes. Among these, vocational programmes are prominent. According to a US Government document, the goal of these programmes in the development of job related skills through a combination of on the job training and class room experience within the institution (LEAA, 1979).

As referred to earlier, Edwin Sutherland has been emphatic about the reformative and rehabilitative value of work by the inmates of jails. The position may not, however, be ignored that the treatment model in institutional correction has itself been questioned. So has been the case with work programmes.

To many scholars, work by the inmates means imposition on them of an additional obligation to work and a restriction on their civil rights (see, for example, Zielinska, 1976). Several other constraints also surface at the operational level. At times, work by jail inmates may be little short of their raw exploitation verging on penal servitude (Sellin, 1967). Owing to several limitations, it may not have, in actual practice, any educational or formative value (see also Lourdjane, 1972). These and similar considerations, thus, have given rise to certain implied goals behind work programmes which are somewhat at variance with the reformatory ideals. These programmes may be regarded as helpful in breaking (dehumanising) new inmates to the jail routine. Many jail functionaries may take them as a means of preventing idleness among the residents.

Notwithstanding this, a number of scholars, adhering to reformatory approach, have laid stress on several underlying purposes behind work. It has a great disciplinary function. "Work is the most reliable means of making an offender accustomed for an orderly and lawabiding life in the community" (Bernhardt, 1969). Secondly, by affording an opportunity to learn new skills, to improve upon the existing ones and to acquire work habits, it develops in the inmates a capacity to become constructive and participative citizens (Carney, 1980). Thirdly, it has a significant resocialisation role. Not only do the inmates learn by doing but, more often than not, they are also required to work in groups situation which brings in its wake the processes of acculturation and re-education through supervised interpersonal interaction. Fourthly, closely associated with work are economic objectives. As is accepted, it is beneficial to the inmate and his dependents as well as to the institution. From these flows the fifth objective: the rehabilitation of the inmates after release (Grant, 1964; Conso, 1973). With the social realism and work skills acquired in the institution, the inmate is likely to readjust easily in the post-release period.

Keeping this backdrop in view, an attempt may be made to see as to what is the perception, at the cutting-edge level, of the objectives behind work.

Staff-viewpoint : On the whole, custodial, treatment and other functionaries in the jail are informed and educated, at least more informed and educated than inmates; and hence, they were in a better position to articulate the purposes underlying

TABLE 5.02

Response of the officials to the question, "With regard to the job/trade assigned to the inmates in this institution, what do you think are the main purposes of such assignment ?"

Purpose	First response	Second response	Weightet score
To maintain order and discipline	72	35	179
To evolve work habits	13	43	69
To provide gainful occupation	03	02	08
To prevent idleness	13	16	42
To achieve self-sufficiency for jail	19	24	62
Total	120	120	360

work by the inmates. A perusal of Table 5.02, nevertheless, brings out more confusion than clarity in this regard : 60% of first the responses and 29.2% of the second responses highlight a non-reformatory purpose, that is, maintenance of order and discipline in the institution. It is, however, gratifying to note that certain reformatory purposes are also mentioned. That work programmes tend to bring the institution closer to self-sufficiency is also underlined by a sizable number of officials. On the whole, the data show that both reformatory and non-reformatory purposes behind work dominate the viewpoint of the functionaries. Further, it would be recalled that the staff sample includes nine vocational instructors as well. What is their perception ? In their first response, all of them have mentioned the prevention of idleness and work habits in the inmates. To a limited extent the divergence in the point of view on the issue between the custodial and treatment practioners is in evidence.

This apart, the possibility of staff members offering normative responses may well be kept in view. As a matter of fact, an overwhelming majority of them accept in principle the rehabilitative value of work programmes (see Table 6.10).

Inmates' viewpoint : Indeed, the inmates are not oriented in the penal philosophy and they are not familiar with abstract considerations underlying work programmes. Nor are they articulate enough to describe intrinsic or long-term objectives. However, their opinion is likely to reflect the policy objectives as percolating down to the field level, into action programmes or conveyed to them by the approach and conduct of the field-level functionaries. This is brought out by the data presented in Table 5.03. Nearly all of them (95.3%) mention an extraneous objective behind work, namely to pass time. Only a few of them mention pertinent purposes. It would be relevant to compare the viewpoint of the staff (Table 5.02) and that of the inmates (Table 5.03). Reformatory objectives behind work are underscored more by the staff than by the inmates. This suggests the existence of a sizable gap between the profession and the practice.

TABLE 5.03

Response of the inmates to the question, "What are the main objectives/purposes behind learning/doing this trade/job?"

	To pass time	To do this job after release	To learn some skill	Total
Frequency	321	03	13	337
Percentage	95.3	0.9	3.9	100

Is it that the inmates, due to certain limitations, are unaware of the purposes underlying work? To answer this question, the data presented in Table 5.03 have been analysed in terms of the personal characteristics of the inmates. Factors like age, caste or education have shown little variation. That work programmes in the institution are governed by non-reformatory ideals is further underlined when the inmate point of view is examined in relation to the time they have put in ($p<.0825$). Furthermore, the viewpoint of the inmates engaged in vocational trades has been examined. Even among these, about 96% of them mention that the objectives is 'to pass time', although the distribution of the data is insignificant. Long-termers, however, seem to have a relatively better appreciation of reformatory objectives ($tau = -0.07349$; $p<0.0217$). Apparently, both traditional nonreformatory and modern and reformatory objectives characterise the organisation of programmes in the institution; furthermore, the former clearly outweigh the latter.

WORK ASSIGNMENT

Assignment to a work unit or trade is an important subroutine of the larger classification procedure in institutional correction. If implemented carefully and systematically, work assignment may facilitate the individualisation of the correctional impact, enable optimum exploitation of their talent and capacity, and further the realisation of correctional objectives. This calls for an amount of deliberation to match the physical and mental potential of the inmates with the available vocational avenues (see Kellerhals, 1959). On the one hand, work programmes need to be attractive, satisfying and relevant and, on the other, they ought to correspond with the interest and capabilities of the inmates (Khan and Unnithan, 1978).

Work Distribution: Keeping the forgoing point in view, a closer look may be had at the work the inmates are doing in the jail. This dimension has already been outlined earlier (Table 5.01); and now it may be probed a little deeper. As work is only a part of the broader treatment strategy, a consideration of the inmates 'participation in other activities like general education and games and sports would not be out of place (Table 5.04). It is found that only 6% of the inmates are attending the jail school; and, likewise, only 17.5% of them participate in games and sports. Further, only two inmates are sport enthusiasts and also school-going. It is significant to note that all of them are engaged in vocational trades. This reinforces the contention that diverse treatment programmes move together and that the permeation of the treatment approach in the institution has to go a long distance.

TABLE 5.04

Participation of the inmates in work, games and school

School	Games	Work: Vocational	Service	Maintenance	Total
No	No	142	38	52	232
	Yes	37	08	07	52
Yes	No	11	—	03	14
	Yes	02	—	01	03
Total		192	46	63	301

Attention may now be turned to the issue whether the work which the inmates are doing corresponds with their personal attributes. There are seen a significant relationship with the age of the inmates (tau=.08218; $p<.0164$). This apart, the education of the inmates also appears to be highly significant related to their work (tau=0.18437; $p<.0001$). Nonetheless, few clear trends are in evidence.

It is worth mentioning that the offence of the inmates shows highly significant difference with the work they are doing ($p<.0051$), the value of rank correlation is negative (tau=—.07807; $p<.0213$). Is offence important in the present context ? Or, is it the term of sentence ? This is what clearly shows up when the inmates, work is analysed in relation to their term of sentence ($p<.0112$), term served ($p<.0001$) and term left ($p<.0506$,), the values of rank correlation are negative (tau=—0.14827; $p<.0001$; tau=—0.13867; $p<.0002$ and tau=—0.06811; $p<.0385$ respectively).

When vocational trades are focalised (N=192), the caste factor appears to be inversely significant (tau= −0.12988; p<.0036). What is more relevant is, however, the offence of the inmate (p<.0198). Vocational trades and the position of convict officers are mostly with the long termers. This broadly confirms to the findings in relation to Central Jail, Madras (Unnithan and Khan, 1979). The time syndrome is highly significant (probability in all the cases is less than .0001).

Process of Assignment : Assignment to a work-unit or to a job in a specific trade is an important sub-routine. In order to maximise the correctional impact of work, the process of assignment needs to be objective and systematic. That in the jail, under study, it is seldom systematic has already been seen. This is supported by the view expressed by one of the nine vocational instructors that it is mainly the manpower requirement which determines the assignment of an inmate to a work or job.

In this context, the opinion of the inmates has also been ascertained. The data presented a little later (Table 5.04) show that barely 6.5% of the inmates had a hand in choosing their work; and in the case of the rest, it had been assigned arbitrarily. The fortunate few who have chosen their work are relatively better-educated (tau=06368; p<.0400). In vocational trades, more than 90% of the inmates have been assigned to the work (p<.0034). In relation to inmate-service, the distribution is not found to be statistically significant.

Is the process of assignment of work to inmates objective ? The opinion of the inmates in this regard has been ascertained earlier (see Tables 2.16 and 2.17). Although a majority of them (85.2%) deny that authorities are partial in assigning a work or a job, a sizable proportion of them (11.6%) think otherwise. Besides, the possibility may well be kept in view that the inmates may not have been forthcoming on the issue. On the whole, there appeared to be much scope for making the process of assignment of work to inmates more systematic and objective.

Work Preference : Work, as also its mode of assignment, is likely to determine the liking or dislike the inmates have for it. In turn, it has implications for the receptivity and impact of the programme. This apart, the liking for a work or job would increase to the extent it comes up to the aspirations, interests and capabilities of the inmates.

On going through Table 5.05, it would be seen that most of the inmates (85.2%) like their present work assignment, but there was a sizable section which disliked it (13.6%). Liking for work, indeed, shows significant differences with the mode of assignment ($p<.0287$). All those who themselves have chosen their work, whether in vocational trades or in inmate service, like it; and all those who dislike their work have been arbitrarily assigned to it. This severely questions the existing practice of bypassing the interests and preference of the inmates in work distribution.

TABLE 5.05

Inmates' liking for the work, work-assignment and the mode of assignment

Work assignment	Mode of assignment	Liking for work			Total
		Dislike	Indifferent	Like	
Vocational	Assigned	12	03	158	173
	Chosen	—	—	19	19
Service	Assigned	13	—	31	44
	Chosen	—	—	02	02
Maintenance	Assigned	15	01	46	62
	Chosen	—	—	01	01
Total		40	04	257	301

In this context, work assignment itself is equally important ($p<.0001$) but the value of rank correlation is negative ($tau=-0.23648$; $p<.0001$). What is more clear is the fact that majority of the inmates engaged in vocational trades like their work. This sub-sample (N=192) has been examined further and the effect of term of sentence on the preferences of the inmates has been ascertained. The term of sentence (tau= 0.08547; $p<.0094$), term served (tau=0.08368; $p<.0107$) and term left ($p<.0317$) are significantly related indicating that the longer the term, the greater the liking the inmates have for their present assignment. This data angle has been persued further. It is found that this kind of work-liking or disliking markedly varies from trade to trade, the distribution as indicated by the value of chi-square is significant (C=0.48398; $p<.0001$). Relatively speaking, all the inmates (100%) in powerloom (N=37), agriculture (N=39), and Baan Kaman (N=4), 97% in spinning and gauze-band age (N=32), 60% in oil-press machine (N=9); 85.7% in weaving (N=30); 92.3% in hand-made paper-making (N=12); 87.5% in tailoring (N=14), shows their work-liking. While in sharp contrast, 40% in oil-press machine (N=6), 14.3% in weaving (N=5), and only 3% in spinning (N=1) dislike their work. Perhaps, there is a case for interfacing this and similar feedback with planning and organisation of work programmes.

What is it that the inmates like in their work ? In this respect, the opinion of all the inmates has been ascertained and about 96% of them have offered information (the presentation of data is deferred). Descending order in terms of frequency of the most attractive features is 'utility' of the job, 'easy' nature of work, instruction/skill and incentives. Further analysis shows that utility, easy nature of work, and skill aspects appeal to the inmates in vocational trades; the easy nature of work and incentives to those in service, and utility and easy nature of work to those in maintenance ($p<.0001$). There are seen a few significant variations within vocational trades themselves ($p<.0001$). For example, the easy nature of work is indicated by those engaged in weaving; utility of work by those in spinning, oil-press machine, papermaking and tailoring, instruction or skill by those in farming and gardening and incentives by those in powerloom and agriculture. Nonetheless, more relevant would be the opinion of those who state that they like their work (Table 5.05). A perusal of Table 5.06 brings out that the order

TABLE 5.06

Most attractive feature of the work as reported by the inmates who like their work and their present work assignment

Features	Work Assignment			Total
	Vocational trades	Service	Maintenance	
Utility	122	09	25	156
Ease	21	19	25	65
Instruction/skill	44	04	06	54
Incentives	02	10	01	13
Total	189	42	57	288

$X^2=91.83165$; $C=0.49170$; df—6; $p<.0001$

of the stated attractive features remains unchanged. So is the case with their appeal to the inmates in different work units.

Before proceeding further, the opinion of the inmates with regard to the least attractive features of their work may be ascertained. As would be seen from the Table 5.07, all the inmates (N=337) have offered information and, among them, more than one-fourth have been meaningless. That the work offered to them in the institution is psychologically unsatisfying, economically unrewarding, unaligned to job avenues available in the outside community and inadequacy of the machines and tools is brought out by the data. Unconducive physical conditions or the ineptness of the work place are also underlined by the majority of the inmates. These responses may be analysed in terms of the present work assignment of the inmates. It is observed ($p<.0001$) that the inmates engaged in vocational trades stress mostly unconducive physical conditions of the work place and inadequate machines and tools in the work units (tau=0.16442; $p<.0002$). If we consider the most and the

TABLE 5.07

Least attractive features of the work being done by the inmates

	Least attractive features					Total
	Unsatis-factory condi-tion	Non-uti-lity of work	Unsatis-factory work	Tools/ machine	Inadequate incentives	
Frequency	118	26	54	08	34	240
Percentage	49.2	10.8	22.5	3.3	14.2	100

least satisfactory feature of the work the inmates are doing in the jail, as perceived by them, it does not take long to see that (a) most inmates know their mind in relation to their work, and (b) measures need to be initiated to recast work-programmes so as to make them more inmate oriented.

Change in assignment : In the situation as it obtains at the field-level, the work assignment of the inmates is subject to change. In other words, they may be shifted from one work-unit to another, for several reasons. Jail authorities may transfer them because of administrative and disciplinary reasons or because of manpower requirements. At times, they may switch the assignment of the inmates following a reclassification as part of larger correctional procedure. Besides, the inmates themselves often desire and opt for a change in their work for several reasons. Whatever the reasons or motivations, a consideration of change in work assignment is important. The linkage between learning and duration is often emphasised. Stated differently, the period of exposure to an educational programme would ordinarily determine the impact it is likely to make on the individual or group. Likewise, willingness to switch assignment, reflects indifference to it on the part of the inmates. To some extent, it may also indicate the preference-pattern the inmates may have for work.

In the institution under study, the classification procedure is

TABLE 5.08

Number of jobs assigned to the inmates in the jail

	One job/ same job	Two jobs	Three jobs	Four or more jobs	Total
Frequency	155	80	49	53	337
Percentage	46	23.7	14.5	15.7	100

itself at best rudimentary However, owing to several administrative and disciplinary reasons, the inmates are moved from one work-unit to another as would be seen from Table 5.08. While 46% of the inmates have been on the job they had begun with, there are more than half of the inmates (54%) who have been on two or more jobs. That this kind of shifting may be related to the time they have spent in the institution, is strongly supported by the highly significant value of rank correlation (tau=0.18707; $p<.0001$). This implies that the inmates who have been in the jail longer have been shifted from one work-unit to another, more than others. Has this kind of shifting anything to do with the present work assignment ? The distribution of the data is significant ($p<.0005$), and shows that the inmates in vocational trades stick to or are allowed to stick to the work or job more than their counterparts in other work units. This is also supported by the highly significant value of rank correlation (tau=0.14112; $p<.0001$).

The reasons for change in work assignment ordered by the jail authorities, may not always be known to the inmates; or else they may not be candid about it. Notwithstanding these constraints, an attempt has been made to ascertain the opinion of the inmates in this regard. About half of the inmates have offered information (due to the smallness of the data, the presentation is deferred). About 44% of the inmates mention the length of the term they had served, and nearly 40% of them, the workshed requirements. It is worth noting that quite a few inmates (15%) regard their shifting from one work-unit to another a disciplinary and administrative measures. Perhaps the work of many an inmate is changed by way of punishment.

In this connection, the views of the inmates with regard to their present work assignment may not be overlooked. It may be found out as to what extent they are willing to stick or to switch their assignment. It is refreshing (Table 5.09) to note that more than three-fourths of the inmates wish to continue with the work they are doing. This may be traced to social as well as situational factors. To elaborate, the time spent in the jail is clearly linked with their preference. Apparently, the greater the amount of time spent in the jail, the more would be the unwillingness to switch the work (tau=0.23950; $p<.0001$). To a considerable extent, the present work assignment is also important in this regard ($p<.0001$). For example, 88% of the inmates in vocational trade are unwilling to switch their work, as against 62% of the inmates engaged in maintenance work. It is, however, important to note that 41.3% of the inmates in service, if permitted, would not hesitate to swap their trade with some other work. This is also supported by the highly inverse significant value of rank correlation (tau= −0.24971; $p<.0001$). Perhaps inter-trade differences are real. This is what becomes evident when attention is focused on the vocational trade subsample (N=192). Whereas the inmates engaged in agriculture, spinning, powerloom, paper-making and tailoring are, by and large, unwilling to leave the trade, those in weaving, oil-press machine and Baan Kaman are ready to do so ($p<.0005$). Besides, a significant relationship is in evidence that the inmates in vocational trades as also in inmate-service ($p<.0213$) who have themselves selected their work are, proportionately are yet not disenchanted with their assignment (the value of rank correlation is tau=0.24271; $p<.0005$).

While on this theme, the job preferences of the inmates may also be explored. Table 5.10 shows that most of the inmates (47.2%) who are willing to switch their job would like to go in for power-loom. Other trades so preferred are agriculture and weaving and tailoring. A few inmates are also willing to do paper-making and oil-press machine. Of greater relevance, however, is the consideration as to what is the advantage the inmates perceive in the job they prefer.

TABLE 5.09

Willingness of the inmates to switch assignment, their present assignment and mode of assignment of their work

Work assignment	Mode of assignment	Willingness to change: Yes	Willingness to change: No	Total
Vocational	Assigned	21	152	173
	Chosen	02	17	19
Service	Assigned	19	25	44
	Chosen	—	02	02
Maintenance	Assigned	24	38	62
	Chosen	—	01	01
Total		66	235	301

TABLE 5.10

Job preferred by the inmates willing to change their work

	Power-loom	Agriculture	Weaving	Tailoring	Paper-making	Oil-press machine	Total
Frequency	34	18	08	06	05	01	72
Percentage	47.2	25	11.1	8.3	6.9	1.4	100

Table 5.11 shows that the inmates relatively know their mind in this regard. Most of them (42%) pointed out that the work they preferred had the learning and utility aspects. Many others (28%) stress that their preference is in line what they were doing before being imprisoned. Quite a few inmates (10%); realists, happy-go-lucky or lethargic, prefer a particular job because it is easy to handle. Finally, it may be remarked that these data-angles, if linked with programme-development, may go a long way towards making it more inmate-oriented.

TABLE 5.11

Reasons given by the inmates for preferring a particular job (percentage).

	Economically useful work, will help afterwards	Prior orientation	Chance to learn new skills	Easy work	Like the work, no reason given	Total	Nothing in particular
First response (N=72)	41.7	27.8	11.1	9.7	9.7	100	(78.6)
Second response (N=8)	37.5	30.5	12.5	—	12.5	100	(97.6)

INFRASTRUCTURAL FACILITIES

In a way, work programmes represent a production-oriented sub-system to which are applicable concepts like direction, time-scheduling, supervision and evalution. Carter *et al.* (1977) recommend such approaches as management by objectives (MBO) and organisation development (OD). They further develop the theme that people are the most effective resource for helping other people. Are these management approaches applicable to correctional institutions ? In terms of management style Likert (1961) has identified four broad categories of institutions : (a) exploitative-authoritative, (b) benevolent-authoritative, (c) participative-consultative, and (d) participative-group. It may be noted that most institutions move from the exploitative-authoritative pattern of management to become participative-group. The Highfield story abundantly illustrates this (McCorkle *et al.*, 1958). Germane, however, is the issue as to where the institution under study stands.

It is difficult to assume that the institution under study has been able to resolve the fundamental conflict between custodial sentence and the idea of reform. It is doubtful that it has been able to reconcile the somewhat opposing policy dictates of individualised treatment of the offender and administrative functions of maintenance of order and security (see also,

Pogrebin, 1974; Reasons and Kaplan, 1975). Indeed, these conflicts and dilemmas appear to have strongly affected the organisation of work programmes as also the provision of requisite infrastructural facilities. Time-scheduling of inputs and organising work programmes using modern management techniques are hardly the *issues.* What, therefore, appears to be appropriate and feasible is that the main facilities like the provision of instructors, equipment, raw-material, etc., may be looked into.

Instructors : The significance of professionals in treatment programmes or of vocational instructors in work programmes can hardly be overestimated. For, these programmes would be a success to the extent they are able to enlist the services of competent and dedicated professionals. Has it been possible ? In the US context, it has been observed that the field (jail service) is unattractive, salaries small, working conditions poor and prestige in public low (the Task Force Report: Corrections, 1967). It is, therefore, hardly surprising that men take up correctional or jail service only as a second or third career choice (Carter *et al.*, 1977).

Conditions obtaining in India are about the same, and even worse, if the position of treatment staff in the jail organisation is considered. A reference to Table 4.09 and 4.10 would show that neither in terms of strength nor status do they occupy any place of importance in the jail hierarchy. As mentioned earlier in this section; all the vocational trades are not provided with instructors separately. Equivalent to a head warder in emoluments and rank, nine are appointed. While on this subject, a few details about these instructors may not be out of place. Out of these nine instructors, 7 are Hindus and rest 2 are Muslims by religion; out of 7 Hindus instructors, 2 are of Brahmins and Kayastha each, and one each of Kshatriya, Vaishya and Schedule Caste. As regards to the distribution of age among the vocational instructors is concerned the average age of the instructors is 40 years. It may be remarked here that the staff can be said to be neither too old nor too young to meet the requirements of job competence. A important consideration in assessing staff-competence is their level of education. This is an enabling factor crucial in orienting staff towards the acceptance of modern methods and techniques of inmate-training. In the institution understudy, nearly half of the instructors have studied high school and above, while rest half of them are under high school level. All of them have been in jail service and on vocational trades for five years or more. With little or no chance for promotion, their post is also somewhat transferable.

Nevertheless, it is gratifying to observe that, despite several personal and organisational limitations, all of the instructors are involved in their work and try to help the inmates. This is what is borne out by the data presented earlier (Table 4.30). About 85% of the inmates feel that they are helpful in teaching them trades. This stands out in sharp contrast when the image of jail authorities, made up mainly of the custodial staff, is examined. A sizable section of the inmates (20%) think that authorities are interested mainly in work and not in the welfare of the inmates. As a matter of fact, a kind of polarity of opinion is observed as far as the perception of the inmates of custodial and vocational staff is concerned, a trend is an evidence that the inmates tend to have distinctly different images of custodial staff and vocational instructors.

Apart from the above, attention may be turned to the training procedure adopted and supervision exercised. It may be formally mentioned that there are no class-room instructions let alone audiovisual aids and the use of other modern techniques for imparting instructions in some of the trades. Whatever the technical skills the inmates pick up they do so through the process of maturation. They begin with manual chores, handle rudiments and, over a period of time, move up to relatively complicated tasks. One of the official US documents be means the poor quality of vocational instruction in institutions (LEAA, 1979). The position in the institution under study is somewhat similar if not worse.

Equipment : In contemporary context, the issue of equipment in relation to work programmes assumes a pointed relevance. The inmates of jails need to learn and do the trades in a way which would be aligned to the pattern of work in the outside community. In several Western correctional institutions certain vocational programmes offered to the inmates need highly sophisticated equipment. Notwithstanding this, there would be few work-units which would not need equipment, simple or otherwise. Even simple chores involving cleaning and sanitation work may require a range of equipment.

What is the position in the jail under study ? Various work-units and factory-sheds in the jail have been outlined earlier. In continuation, it may be stated that the maintenance unit does not have much by way of equipment except for broomsticks, baskets and a few hand-barrows. In the inmate-service, barbers of course have their kit. The work in the kitchen is traditional (except for the flour mill) needing hardly any equipment. The gadgets in different vocational trades have already been referred to. In any case there is little of importance to describe.

Apparently, mechanisation is yet to attract the attention of decision-makers. In Lucknow region, agriculture has been modernised considerably. Apart from the use of improved seeds, fertilizers and pesticides, farmers are using tractors and harvesters. Powerlooms are common not only in cloth making but also in carpet and durri making. To great extent, such equipments are also available in the jails' agriculture and powerloom work-units, but the maintenance of these equipments is not adequate or sufficient. This apart, some amount of mechanisation is also possible in inmate service and the maintenance unit : two typewriters for those inmates attached to the office, a washing machine for those in the laundry, and baking equipment for those in the kitchen. However, the jail authorities do not appear to have felt the need to introduce mechanisation in these work programmes in the jail.

Keeping this in view, the opinion of the inmates in respect of the provision of equipment has been assessed (Table 5.12). Only 10.6% of the inmates have reservations in this regard; and the rest of the inmates (89.3%) seem to be satisfied. Interestingly enough, the opinion of the inmates is significantly and positively

TABLE 5.12

Responses of the inmates to the question, "For the job/trade that you are doing, are you provided with the necessary machinery?"

	No	Can't say	Yes	Total
Frequency	18	18	301	337
Percentage	5.3	5.3	89.3	100

related to their job liking (tau=0.12076; $p<.0005$) and to their unwillingness to switch the job (tau=0.08738; $p<.0082$). It may, however, be noted that the inmates in vocational trades are not so much satisfied with the equipment they have been provided.

The inmates are, however, expressing their opinion from the perspective they have. The provision of equipment is not only a matter of 'felt need' but also of 'created need'. This aside, the aspect relating to the maintenance of the equipment may not be sufficiently clear to them. As such, the view of the nine instructors has been ascertained. They have expressed some encouraging opinions : to seven, the provision of equipment is adequate, and to the rest, 'so-so', and the same distribution is seen regarding the condition of the equipment. Indeed, in the opinion of the inmates, there appears to be much scope for bringing about a quantitative as well as qualitative change in the equipment and machinery for different work units in the jail under study.

Raw-Material : Yet another important input in work programmes is raw material. While describing work-units and vocational trades early in this section, this aspect has been briefly touched upon. It would be recalled that agricultural inputs like improved seeds and fertilizers are purchased through the District Agriculture Department. Likewise, for weaving, spinning and power-loom sections, yarn and dye are centrally purchased mostly from Kanpur and supplied to the jail. There are few other units or vocational trades requiring the supply of any specific raw-material. It may be remarked here that all the sale or purchase of goods produced in the jail, are done by the Jail Depot, Lucknow, in open market.

Indeed, the inmates cannot be expected to offer information about the adequacy or the quality of raw-material supplied to different vocational trades. Nevertheless their opinion on these issues can hardly ignored. It is seen (Table 5.13) that most of the inmates (86.9%) feel that factory-sheds are getting adequate raw-material. However, there is a sizable section of them (13%) which has reservations about it. On the above point in view, liking for jobs, significantly related (tau=0.12076; p<.0005), is strong supporting. Apart from this, the work which the inmates

TABLE 5.13

Response of the inmates to the question, "Eor the job/trade that you are doing, are you yetting adequate raw material ?"

	No	Can't say	Yes	Total
Frequency	09	35	293	337
Percentage	2.7	10.4	86.9	100

are doing appears to influence their opinion (p<.0001). The inmates in vocational trades as compared with those in other work units have a favourable view. It may be inferred that the supply of raw-material where it matters is not wholly satisfactory. Interestingly, the eight out of nine vocational instructors were categorical during formal interview that the supply of raw-material in different vocational trade is adequate. In sharp contrast, several jail officials, including one vocational instructor (during formal interview) in the course of informal interaction during data-collection, have been critical about it. Notwithstanding the rules and regulations governing purchase and supply of stores, the raw-material supplied to the factory-sheds, in the opinion of many officials, is of low quality. Perhaps this issue needs further investigation.

Distribution : Focusing attention on work programmes, in general, and on vocational trades in particular, it is justifiable to regard them as representing a production subsystem. It follows that a production sub-system yields optimum results when organised along professional lines. There are many writers who emphasise that jail industries need to be run on the principles and using the techniques of business management. In any case, any production unit would be seldom content with inputs and production alone; attention has to be paid to distribution and sales aspects. This is not without justification. Properly organised distribution and sales are likely to generate profits and surplus which would, in turn, give impetus to enhanced investment on these activities and for devising a realistic incentive scheme for the inmates.

In the United States, the Prison Industries Corporation (Prind) has been set up to regulate not only the supply of raw-materials to factory sheds in different correctional institution but also to organise the distribution and sale of produce through commercial outlets. A similar step has been taken in the State of Uttar Pradesh : the U.P. Jail Industries Corporation has been set up. It is commonly known as Jail Depot, headquartered at Lucknow.

In the jail under study, whatever the quantity of goods produced, is consumed or sold to the customers through Jail Depot, Lucknow. For example, in 1976, Jail Depot, Lucknow, sold goods produced in the institution worth of Rs. 2,26,134. It may be noted that the costing of goods produced does have a guideline. The sale price is variable : for private persons—cost +30%; institutions, including government department—cost+ 20%; and jail department, including jail officials—cost+10%. It may be pointed out that government departments have instructions to give preference to jail produce. This apart, purchases from jails avoid cumbersome official procedure of tenders, quotations and so on. Keeping in view the position of production, distribution and sale of jail produce, as they obtain at present, it is difficult to say that all is satisfactory. This apart, the contention is further reinforced that work programmes are yet to be accorded the priority they deserve.

Incentives : While analysing the reasons behind the failure of different jail industries, the US President's Commission on Law Enforcement and Administration of Justice, 1967, laid emphasis on the fact that, more often than not, work incentives were unsatisfactory or meagre. Similarly, Halleck stresses the need "to provide prisoners with realistic incentives" (1967). The term 'incentive' may be taken to denote a material or non-material stimulus made available to inmates towards enlarging their participation in work and thereby increasing their output (Unnithan and Khan, 1978; Trivedi, 1977). In this connection, both formal and informal incentives as also negative (punishment) and positive (reward) incentives are often brought up (Maier, 1965).

Armstrong (1950) indicates several prerequisites for a good incentive system as follows : (a) Employee-orientation : An incentive scheme may have understandable and calculable benefits for the employee. It should be used to gain their confidence; (b) Employer-orientation : The incentive system needs to be beneficial to the organisation in that it should have the capacity to remain operable under extreme market conditions; not be very costly; and should control and assist supervision as well as stimulate co-operation and interest in the wellbeing of the organisation; (c) performance-orientation : Lastly, incentive ought to have a linkage with effort. It should stimulate those characteristics in the employee which the organisation wishes to improve. While these postulates have been laid down with commercial organisations in view, most of them hold good for industries in correctional institutions as well.

Punishment as negative incentives may range from reprimand, public or private, cancellation of remission or corporal punishment and withholding of certain previleges and benefits. Also, they have been outlined in the Prisons Act of 1894 (section 48). Nonetheless, the significance of punishment as a means to stimulate inmate performance has seldom been sufficiently realised.

In the Italian context, Conso (1973) strongly pleads for a meaningful and fair remuneration to the inmates who work in the factorysheds. Notwithstanding the Italian situation, in most countries on the Continent, inmates who participate in productive work are paid judicious wages—part of which may be paid immediately and the balance credited to their account to be paid to them at the time of their release. In Canada, in most jails, the inmates are provided wages which may not necessarily compare with those outside in the community, but in no case are they below 20% (McGrath, 1965). Almost the same is the position in the United States. In most reformatories and penitentiaries, inmates are paid regular wages and sometimes bonus or 'premium' is remitted to their dependents (Brando, 1967).

In India, bidi, additional 'good days' or remission and appointment as convict officer are the main non-material incentives offered to the inmates. In most of jails, wage schemes do not exist, and in some the inmates are paid token wages. On the other hand, like open jails, and the institution under study, also have the provision for regular and comparable wages to the inmates.

Punishment: The moot question, however, is whether punishment is used, whatever the frequency, to improve their work performance. Eight out of nine vocational instructors state that the inmates whose work or performance is found unsatisfactory are given punishment including reprimand, forfeiture or cancellation of remission and even transfer from one to another unit. It is further supported by the opinion of the inmates in this regard. More than three-fourths of the inmates (80%) state that in relation to unsatisfactory work in factory sheds, punishment was given (presentation of data is deferred). On the other hand, a sizable section of the inmates (20%) had reservation in this regard.

Notwithstanding the above, an attempt may be made to see as to what the main forms of punishment awarded to defaulting inmates were. About 80% of the inmates offered information on the issue (see Table 5.14), Frequent methods, as reported by the inmates, include both soft and severe forms of punishment. It may be noted that nearly three-fourths of the inmates report punishment as cancellation of remission. Beside this, putting an inmate in solitary confinement is major punishment which usually result as a sequel to serious problems of behaviour and conduct. There is hardly a possibility of these punish-

TABLE 5.14

Response of the inmates to the question, "If one's performance in the trade/job is found by the officials to be unsatisfactory, is he given punishment ? If yes, what is it ?"

	Cancellation of remission	Solitary confinement	Oral reprimand	Caning	Link and fetters	Transfer from one trade to another	Total
Frequency	195	24	17	15	10	06	267
Percentage	73	9	6.4	5.6	3.7	2.2	100

ments being awarded in relation to work performance. Seemingly, the context has not been sufficiently clear to the inmates; or else, performance or non-performance in factory sheds is not a matter of any great official concern.

Appreciation : Formal or informal recognition, including praise and appreciation, especially from superiors, is "a vital form of ego-satisfaction" (Maier, 1965), which, if used discerningly, may perceptibly improve work performance of the praised. In the present study, an attempt has been made to look into both informal and formal aspects. Table 5.15 brings out the opinion of the inmates about the appreciation or praise they receive for their above-average work performance. The positive opinion of the inmates in this regard may be a little parsimonious; yet it is gratifying that nearly 41% of them report about their performance being appreciated (see also Unnithan and Khan, 1978). Notice, however, needs to be taken of the fact that more than half (about 59%) of them report in the negative. This hardly speaks well of the staff or its therapeutic orientation.

TABLE 5.15

Response of the inmates to the question, "Whenever you have done hard work or show above average performance, have the authorities appreciated, or praised it ?"

	No	Don't remember	Yes	Total
Frequency	198	02	137	337
Percentage	58.8	0.6	40.7	100

As would be expected, the inmates who are better educated ($p<.0001$), and are aware of purposes behind work ($tau=0.06937$; $p<.0283$), are appreciated more than others—but only marginally so. Likewise, time-related variables, including length of sentence ($tau=0.07781$; $p<.0162$), term served ($tau=-0.07727$; $p<.0168$), and term left ($tau=0.05217$; $p<.0758$)—all significantly and directly vary with the inmates' opinion. Perhaps with the passage of time, the inmates are able to put up better performance and to receive appreciation. Further, the inmates in vocational trade are somewhat better off than those in inmate service and in maintenance work, report that their performance is appreciated and praised ($tau=-0.15234$; $p<.0001$). A few tradewise differences are also noticed ($p<.0021$) : the work of the inmates in weaving and power-loom sections is appreciated more than of those in other trades. All this apart, the basic question remains : Is this most inexpensive form of incentive used sufficiently ?

The award of diplomas or certificates has been recommended by the First UN Congress (1955) as an integral part of prison labour programmes. Indeed, the procedure has many possibilities: it may encourage inmates to added effort, introduce an element of healthy competitiveness and bring about a qualitative change in their performance. Concerning the jail under study, provision do not exist, and none of the inmates is a recipient of any diploma, certificate or medal. Probably, jail authorities regard the procedure irrelevant.

Benefits and Privileges: Apart from the remission in sentence of two days in a month admissible to all the inmates with satisfactory conduct and behaviour, the inmates who work in vocational trades are given an additional remission of two days. In some jails in the country, they are also provided with such facilities such as *bidi*, ration (Unnithan and Khan, 1978). As mentioned earlier, wages or even comparable wages are also offered, like the open jails. Besides, the inmates who put up above average performance are elevated to positions like the change of Bhawans in onwards gradation (Jamuna bhawan→Ganga→Bihari); or the chance of being promoted to convict officers (night watchman, overseer or warder); or they may be put in charge of work-squads. These positions also carry certain official and unofficial privileges, such as separate dining arrangement, special remission, etc., to the inmates. Four good days or remission in a month are allowed to most inmates as a matter of routines.

Elevation to the position of convict officer, as mentioned earlier, depends on many considerations, and hard work and performance in a work-unit or vocational trade may be or is only one of them. This partly explains why only 19% of the inmates feel that good conduct and record is considered for the promotion of convict officers. While on the other, more than three-fourths (80%) of them state that through or by seniority or time served in jail, they can reach the position of convict officers (representation of data is deferred). Apparently, there is a case to link up performance with promotions and to streamline the procedure for appointing convict officers.

The importance of wages, whatever the 'reference scale' (Bernhardt, 1969), in motivating inmates to better performance has been outlined earlier. Wenk and Frank (1973) have collected empirical evidence showing that cash incentives are instrumental in changing certain inmate behaviour, is more or less

TABLE 5.16

Response of the inmates to the question, "If instead of remission in your sentence you are given wages, would you prefer it ?"

	No	Can't say	Yes	Total
Frequency	269	07	61	337
Percentage	79.8	2.1	18.1	100

proportionate to the amount paid. In this connection, the opinion of the vocational instructors in the jail under study has been ascertained. Out of nine instructors, five are of opinion that remission as an higher incentive than wages. On the other hand, rest of the four instructors rate wages as an higher incentive than remission. What is the opinion of the inmates in this regard? A reference of Table 5.16 would show that about 80% of the inmates do not favour the idea of remission being supplemented by wages. Interestingly, their opinion varied with their work assignment ($p<.0087$): those in inmate-service followed by those in vocational trades were comparatively more in favour of wages than others. The value of rank correlation is also highly supported ($tau=0.14642$; $p<.0001$). At this stage, it may be clarified that rarely do the wages, almost everywhere, supplant remission-they supplement it. In a production subsystem having a profit-orientation, the principle of profit sharing is difficult to be side-tracked. That is how the inmates in vocational trades also feel, as ascertained during informal conversation. It may be remarked that in any systematic reorganisation of work-programmes, the provision of cash-incentives or wages to the inmates need to be given due attention.

In retrospect, it may be stated that work programmes in the jail have much scope for modification and innovation. Organisational policies and priorities, dominated apparently by the nineteenth century notions of custody and security, were in effect indifferent towards the significance and efficacy of work programmes. Consequently, the range of vocational trades available to the inmates was as much outdated as it was small. Besides, 36.2% of the labour of inmates is frittered away on inmate-service and maintenance having doubtful rehabilitative value, and only, 63.8% of them are put on vocational trades. Notwithstanding the fact that an overwhelming proportion of the inmates was from rural areas and with a agrarian background, only 20.3% were engaged in farming, and, of course, still mechanisation was somewhat less thought of. This aside, there were some other trades like, spinning and weaving, where some indifferent mechanisation was introduced. The need for modernisation and diversification of trades appeared to be imperative. The ambiguity in policies and priorities governing work programmes was correspondingly reflected in their manifest or underlying purposes as perceived by the inmates and officials. Their response-pattern reminds one of the nineteenth century prisons and penitentiaries.

The organisation of work programmes is in no way the only victim of official indifference. Almost the same is the case with other programmes and procedures. The classification system in operation is not much systematic and no conscious and meaningful procedure is adopted to assign inmates to different work-units or trades. Rarely does the educational background of the inmates or their occupational antecedents, and much less their aptitude, constitute a criterion in the assignment procedure. In this regard the inmates' work preferences also seem to be muddled.

More than three-fourth (85.2%) of them like their job and at the same time, nearly 21.4% of the inmates are willing to switch it. However, they do know their mind, as indicated by the advantages they mention of the work they would like to change it.

Also, the infrastructure available for work programmes leaves much to be desired. Not only are the background and status of vocational instructors inadequate but also many trades do not have the post. Needless to say, the equipment in most factory sheds is absolete and its maintenance indifferent. The supply of raw material, whatever its inventory, is circuitous and procedure-bound and hence of indifferent quality. Likewise, little concerted attention has been paid to the establishment of viable outlets for the produce from the factory sheds.

Most wanting, however, are the motivations or incentives of offered to the inmates. The word of appreciation or praise, which costs nothing, has been used only sparingly. Medals or certificates were unheard of. The inmates, whether in vocational trades or in other workunits, were given unrealistic remuneration or wages. The less durable and negative incentive, punishment, appeared to be frequent, as about 80% of the inmates mention it. All things considered, there was little evidence to suggest that the work programmes in the Model Jail, in their organisation and working, were purposive or inmate—oriented. The hypothesis almost explicitly remains unsubstantiated.

6

The Impact

Programme evaluation in corrections faces several methodological problems. Both input and output are not easy to conceptualise or define. The multiplicity of intervening, often unexplained, variables is large. Likewise, informants may not be always available or cooperative. A developing country like India may suffer from yet another handicap : the resource constraint.

Nevertheless, evaluation of various correctional programmes with varying degrees of investment and success has been attempted. For example, Bailey (1966) has looked into 100 evaluation reports so as to determine correctional outcome. The effectiveness of prison and borstal system has also been assessed (see Fox, 1952; Glaser, 1964). Witte and Reid (1980) report that inmates after their release face many difficulties in landing a job. Hulin (1959) has enquired into the changes in the attitude towards law concomitant with imprisonment, while Hodgkin (1972) has measured the impact of special projects involving team work on the part of residents of a correctional institution. A comprehensive review of evaluation literature has been provided by Lipton et al (1975).

In relation to correctional institutions in India, evaluatory studies are few and far between. Nor is there any regular institutional arrangement for this. Of course, a large number of commissions, committees and study groups appointed by the Central and State Governments have touched upon this aspect. They have, however, proceeded more on the basis of impressionistic account than on empirical data.

In a limited way, the present section attempts to assess the impact of work programmes on the inmates in the Model Jail, Lucknow. This could have been best achieved by focussing attention on the inmates released from the institution and by looking into the extent to which they have been able to readjust into their community. Nonetheless, some meaningful information is possible to collect which to a good deal may reflect the impact. This contention partially finds support from the position taken by Lipton et al (1975) that the effectiveness of a treatment programme is possible to assess on the basis of institutional adjustment, changes in the attitude pattern and achievement, on the one hand, and recidivism, drug readdiction and adjustment in the community, on the other. For the present purposes, attention has been focused on the former.

It is often argued that owing to several personal factors many inmates were unable to benefit from instructional programmes. On the other hand, in recent decades, evidence had been piling up to show that the jail routine and atmosphere were a drag. These issues are worth highlighting. Adhering to an *ex post facto* approach, the present section proceeds to examine a descriptive hypothesis : *The positive impact of work programmes on inmates is determined more by the offence and work-related factors than by personal factors.* It may be clarified that age, religion, caste, education and family background are regarded as personal factors; offence and term of imprisonment, as offence-related variables. Work assignment, liking of work and so forth, as work-related factors. This aside, the impact is proposed to be assessed in terms of role perception, skill development, involvement in work and the like. Further, inmates engaged in vocational trades are proposed to be compared with those in other work units.

ROLE PERCEPTION

To what extent the residents in the institution under study have been able to bring about an adjustment between themselves and the officials, has been outlined in Chapter Two. A reference has also been made to appreciation, reward and punishment received by them (see also, Trivedi, 1980). In so far as vocational adjustment is concerned, the preceding section brings under focus such aspects as understanding of the purpose behind work and liking for the job. Taken together, these aspects reveal a somewhat mixed position : The level of adjustment is high in some inmates and low in others. Basic to institutional adjustment is the concept of role perception (see Hulin, 1959; Reinhardt, 1968; Peretti, 1969). It would be justifiable to presume that role perception is a relatively enduring psycho-social entity which comes about over a period of time through experiences and exposure of treatment programmes. It may greatly influence the participation as also the involvement of the inmates in all the intra-mural activities. In order to assess the nature of role perception by the inmates, attention has been focused mainly on two dimensions : role identification and role adherence.

Role identification : Entering the jail and joining a work unit marks a radical break from the past routine roles and responsibilities. To a good deal a given inmate would be able to benefit from work programmes to the extent he is able to adjust with his new surroundings and identify with his new roles. Many an inmate was given to lethargy or inertia. He may be given to the idea that the institution or his work unit would continue to function somehow whether or not he participated. The past traumatic experiences may weigh heavy on him and he may suffer from a feeling of worthlessness. This may hamstring his participation in institutional activities in no small way. Owing to a variety of reasons, the work assigned to him may be less than satisfying. Then, most vocational trades require concerted effort and team work. An insufficient understanding of this requirement may heavily tell both on the uptake of skills and production in the factory shed. These are some of the issues which have been explored.

TABLE 6.01

Role identification by the inmates (Percentages).

Statements	Responses		
	Agree	Can't say	Disagree
In your karkhana/unit where you and others work, it would not matter if one person does not work. (N=337)	73	11.6	15.4
No matter what amount of effort you make but the quality of goods produced/work done in your karkhana/unit is not going to improve much (N=337)	41.2	26.4	32.3
The work in karkhana/unit allows an inmate to show his talent (N=337)	80.7	9.2	10.1
The work in karkhana/unit will get upset if all do not work together. (N=337)	94.4	3.6	2.1

On going through Table 6.01, it would be seen that nearly three-fourths of the inmates were given to lethargy and felt that it hardly mattered whether a person works or not in the karkhana or unit. This data position was far from encouraging. This apart, among personal factors, only education of the inmates showed significant variation ($p<.022$) with this dimension. On the other hand, among the offence-related variables, only term served ($p<.0006$) are positively associated with the inmates opinion, the inmates who had still many more years to serve, tended to disagree with the statement. It is inferred that these inmates were less given to lethargy. Attention may now be turned to work-related variables. Present work assignment ($p<.022$) as well as the number of jobs handled by the inmates show a significant difference ($p<.0001$). Relatively speaking, the inmates in vocational trades regarded and took their work seriously and those who have been time and again shifted from job to job, took it easy. This aside, liking for the present job (tau= —0.08897; $p<.0072$) and willingness to change the present job show the highly significant but inverse association (tau= —0.06058; $p<.0480$) with this dimension. Instructors helpful in teaching the jobs also showed a good deal of inverse relationship (tau= —0.12310; $p<.0004$) with this statement.

The second statement in Table 6.01 attempts to assess the sense of vocational efficacy of the inmates in their respective karkhana/unit. It is refreshing to note that 32.3% of the inmates possesses a high level of self-esteem and that less than half (41.2%) of them saw no scope of improvement in their karkhana/unit no matter what efforts they make. Probably, most inmates were involved in their work. This aside, few personal factors had a bearing on their opinion. So is not, however, the case with offence-related variables. For example, the inmates convicted for murder, robbery and dacoity showed relatively a high sense of vocational efficacy ($p<.0023$). Similar is the position of long termers. Still more notable differences were seen in relation to work-related variables. Those in vocational trades (76%) and inmate service (24%) showed a high sense of vocational efficacy. A few inter-trade differences were also noticed. The inmates in power-loom, weaving, spinning and farming were better off in this respect than others. Incidentally, the place in vocational unit is significantly related to this ($c=.48272$; $p<.0001$). This apart, achievement level in vocational training shows a good deal of relationship ($p<.0202$), the value of rank correlation is significantly linked (tau=—0.10723; $p<.0016$) with this issue. It may be remarked that the sense of vocational efficacy is clearly influenced more by work related factors than others.

Next, attention has been turned to work satisfaction the inmates have in their karkhana/unit. Their response has been elicited on the item, "The work in the karkhana/unit allows an inmate to show his talents" (Table 6.01). It is encouraging to note that more than three-fourths of the inmates were positive in this regard. At the same time, the fact may not be overlooked that a sizable section (10.1%) of the inmates feel otherwise. Apparently, work assignment was not properly matched with inmate background and aptitude. What is it that influences inmate opinion ? Few personal factors of the inmates show any significant difference in this regard. Among offence-related variables, offence itself shows a negative but significant association (tau= —0.05677; $p<.0593$) along with term served ($p<.0001$). Relatively speaking, the inmates who were in the institution longer, tended to agree that the work allowed an inmate to show his talent (tau=.14999; $p<.0001$). In sharp contrast, several work-related variables were found to be highly significant. For example, work assignment showed a good deal of significant but inverse relationship with this dimension (tau= —0.19281; $p<.0001$). It is worth noting that the attitude of the inmates towards their vocational instructors was significantly related to this (tau= .08768; $p<.008$), that is to say, the inmates who have found vocational instructors helpful in teaching them the trade, feel that the work affords an opportunity for the expression of their talents. Again, job-liking of the inmates appears to be important in this regard (tau=.26653; $p<.0001$), followed by willingness to change of present job (tau= .21788; $p<.0001$) is also highly significant with this dimension. It would be thus justifiable to suggest that work-related factors have a substantial and positive influence on the level of work satisfaction of the inmates.

The importance of *esprit de corps* in a production-oriented sub-system can hardly be discounted. It is important in all work units but it is crucial in vocational trades. This is what has been sought to be ascertained through the statement, "The work in the karkhana/unit will get upset if all do not work together" (see Table 6.01). It would be seen that an overwhelming majority of the inmates (94.4%) were aware of the value of team work. Owing to this kind of skewed distribution no attempt was made at further analysis. This apart, the foregoing analysis brings out that by and large inmates do identify their role and that, in this aspect relating to their work in the institution have a decisive influence.

Role adherence : The identification of roles or new roles is one thing, and abiding by them is another. Since role identification is often times ideatory, many inmates would be aware of them or even profess them. However, due to several internal or external reasons, they may not always adhere to them. In any case, adherence to role by the inmates may indirectly provide an estimate of the impact of work programmes. With this in view, an attempt has been made to assess as to how far they have been able to adhere to the roles they themselves consider to be important (see Chapter Three). Further, as their opinion with regard to their own role adherence may not be wholly objective, or dependable, the viewpoint of the officials has also been ascertained.

TABLE 6.02

Responses of the officials to the question, "Among the inmates participating satisfactorily in the work programmes have you noticed any positive change in their behaviour ?"

	No	In some cases	Yes	Total	NR
Frequency	—	91	27	120	2
Percentage	—	77.1	22.9	100	(1.7)

Table 6.02 brings out the opinion of the officials with regard to the impact of work programmes on the general behaviour of the inmates. Seemingly, their opinion is encouraging but is divided : more than three-fourths of them have reservations and among the rest about 23% of the officials hold a positive opinion. In the view of the officials, the impact of work programmes on the general behaviour of the inmates is mostly encouraging and positive. The issue needs to be examined a little more closely.

In order to assess the role adherence of the inmates three questions have been asked from the inmates. Although the referent in these questions is the inmate population in general, it is assumed that the inmates would be speaking in the light of their own experience. These very questions have been asked from the jail officials (see Table 6.03). On the issue of giving no occasion to jail authorities to get displeased, the opinion of the officials appeared to be better than the inmates themselves.

TABLE 6.03

Role adherence by the inmates as ascertained from the inmates and the officials (percentage).

Statement	Sample	Response		
		None of them	Some of them	Most of them
Do you think that inmates complete their sentence giving jail authorities no occasion to get displeased?	(Inmate) 337	3.9	43.5	52.6
	(Staff) 120	4.2	33.3	62.5
Do you think that inmates use the time in jail towards improving their ideas and conduct ?	(Inmate) 337	2.1	20	77.9
	(Staff) 120	4.2	34.2	61.7
Do you think that inmates work hard without bothering about remission or reward ?	(Inmate) 337	7.4	50.7	41.8
	(Staff) 120	8.3	80.8	10.8

While 62.5% of the officials mentioned that most of the inmates completed their term of sentence without giving an occasion to them to be displeased, on the other hand more than half (52.6%) of the inmates thought so. Does this reflect impact of treatment programmes or vigorous discipline enforced in the jail ? Apart from this issue, the response pattern speaks well of the inmate-staff relationship and of the institutional adjustment of the inmates. This contention is further strengthened by the fact that the officials who were better educated ($p<.0001$) were found to be more positive on this ($tau=0.18167$; $p<.0015$).

The linkage of influencing factors may be examined. Personal factors of the inmates are found in no way connected with this. Among the offence-related variables, term of imprisonment is found to be significant with this ($tau=0.06505$; $p<0.0382$), this is followed by the term served and term left ($p<.0001$ in each case). As regards the work-related variables, most of these were found to be highly significant relationship with this dimension. However, for example, trade assignment of the inmates was highly significant in this regard ($p<.0102$). Relatively speaking, the inmates engaged in agriculture (21%) followed by those in power-loom (20%) and in weaving (19%) think that most of them behave to the satisfaction of the authorities. Interestingly enough, the opinion of the inmates that vocational instructors were helpful in teaching them the trade ($tau=-0.08683$; $p<.009$), their job was likable ($tau=-0.14883$; $p<.0001$) and that their willingness to change their jobs ($tau=-0.16933$; $p<.0001$) was negative. Apparently, the inmates who were involved in work were much critical of fellow residents. Alternatively, they may be less than satisfied with superficial obeisance which was more or less routine in the jail.

Do the inmates cooperate towards their own reformation ? The second question in Table 6.03 brings out the relevant information. The response pattern of the inmates is much encouraging than the officials. Still, more than half (61.7%) of the officials thought that the inmates use the time in jail towards improving their ideas and conduct. At the same time, it is difficult to bypass this data position. The officials who are mature in service ($p<.0121$), who are more educated ($tau=.18083$; $p<.0016$), who like their job ($p<.0196$) and who enjoy interaction with the inmates ($tau=0.78119$; $p<.0001$) thought along this line.

In every case, the opinion of inmates is much encouraging. More than three-fourths of them thought that most of their brethern were interested in reforming themselves or improving their ideas and conduct. Further few personal variables or offence related variables were found to be significantly important in this regard. Among work-related variables, interestingly enough, the opinion of the inmates that vocational instructors were helpful in teaching them trade (tau= —0.04998; p<.0870) and that their purpose behind work (tau= —0.11191; p<.0012) was negative. On the overall response pattern of the officials and the inmates on this dimension, it would be inferred that the reformation of the inmates in the jail was in a very happy position.

What about role adherence vis-a-vis work in the jail ? This is what has been sought to be ascertained through the third item in Table 6.03. The opinion of the officials was mostly negative. While 8.31% of them thought that no inmate works hard without bothering about remission or reward, only 10.8% thought to the contrary. Their opinion appeared to be related to their education (tau= .22292; p<.0001) as also to their job liking (tau= .15000; p<.0071) and the correction orientation (tau= .35011; p<.0001). This implied that the officials who were educated and who enjoyed correctional work were better disposed towards inmates than others.

As regards the linkage of other variables with the opinion of the inmates about selfless working, extensive cross-analysis has been carried out. But few personal factors have shown any significant difference. The offence for which the inmates have been convicted shows a significantly inverse association with this (tau= —0.07556; p<0.0189) followed by term of sentence (tau=0.04843; p<.0916) and has a negative relationship with term served (tau= —0.09734; p<.0037). Several work-related variables, including mode of trade-assignment (p<.0361), number of job handled (tau= —0.09552; p<.0043), job liking (p<.0052), unwillingness to swap work (tau= —0.07636; p<.0179) and instructors helpful in teaching them trades (p<.0001) show significant differences. That aspect relating to work as compared with others are much important, is amply brought out by the data.

SKILLS AND ACHIEVEMENTS

Do the inmates acquire work skills ? As mentioned earlier, many writers contend that they are lethargic, malingers and unteachable because of illiteracy, incapacity and similar other personal factors. However, it would be unrealistic to assume that only personal factors are a barrier in the acquisition of work skills. Even after including such subtle personal factors like aptitude, interest and capability, there are many other factors which have a critical bearing (see Khan and Unnithan, 1978). A work programme to be effective needs to be aligned not only to individual personality needs but also to the outside labour market. Training environment is equally important. Work place, equipments, instructors and the quality of instructions—all are likely to influence the acquisition of the skills and the level of achievements by inmates (Unnithan and Khan, 1979). In this respect, the importance of the incentives can hardly be overemphasized.

The factors which are likely to influence the acquisition of skills by the inmates and their achievement level have been outlined in the preceding section. It is justifiable to state that most of these enabling factors have been found to be less than satisfactory. Nonetheless, an attempt to assess directly skill development amongst the inmates may not be out of place. This should aid in developing a better understanding of the institution as well as of the inmates. Further, it is likely to have implications for the implementation of work programmes at the institutional level.

Acquisition of skills : Apart from the limiting conditions outlined above, yet another factor, namely the understanding and awareness of the purpose behind work, may well be kept in view. As shown in Chapter Five, most of the officials and the inmates mention traditional and nonreformatory objectives. This may have far-reaching implications for skill development. Hence, an attempt may be made to ascertain the quality of participation by the inmates in different work-programmes.

In this connection, it may well be kept in mind that the willing participation in an activity, especially a production-oriented work, is markedly different from forced participation. On the other hand, assignment to and participation in some work or the other by the inmates is routine in the jail. It would be thus relevant to probe into the views of the officials as to whether the inmates are really interested in work or else they participate because it is an institutional routine.

On going through Table 6.04, it would be seen that the view of the officials with regard to inmate participation in work programme is far from being bright. Barely, 5.8% of them indicate that the inmates are earnest about work. The officials may be given to predisposed opinion yet their proportion holding a negative opinion is much too large to be ignored.

TABLE 6.04

Response of the officials to the question, "Do you feel that inmates participate willingly in work programmes or because they have to ?"

	They have to	Willingly	Total
Frequency	113	07	120
Percentage	94.2	5.8	100

This data position, however, may well not be appraised in isolation. As indicated earlier, interest and participation in a given work or trade coupled with its being interesting, satisfying and aligned to work in the outside community. A perusal of Table 6.05 would show that barely 13% of the inmates have been assigned work in the jail which somewhat corresponds with what they were doing before their conviction. Have they learned anything new ? Very few or a negligible number of

TABLE 6.05

Showing the response of the inmates to the question, "If the job/trade is same as done outside, have you learnt anything new here ?"

	No	Yes	NA	Total
Frequency	42	01	294	337
Percentage	12.5	0.3	87.2	100

them respond in the affirmative. This reinforces the earlier contention that the work or trade which matches with the inmate background mostly include agriculture, laundary and hair-cutting. It would also be recalled that in quite a few vocational trades and inmate service, little or no effort is made at conscious skill development among the inmates. It is, therefore, hardly surprising that so very few inmates report to have learnt anything new.

In the subsequent analysis the inmates in the category of not applicable has been omitted. It is found that personal factors of the inmates have no association with their learning or not learning of new skills. The time syndrome, however, is found to be important. The trend is that the inmates who have a longer term of sentence ($p < .0014$) and have been in the jail for long ($p < .0014$) are more likely to find something new in the work. Among work-related variables, only the number of jobs handled by the inmates ($p < .0508$) and willingness to change the job ($p < .0292$) show significant differences with this. Since the value of rank correlation of willingness to change of job is negative ($tau = -0.69864$; $p < .0001$), it appears that many inmates following some amount of experimentation and clamouring do land a job offering something new.

Closely related is the issue of the perceived utility of the work/trade if it happens to be different from what the inmates were doing before coming to the jail. Data presented in Table 6.06 throw light on this dimension. It is seen that 64.3% of the inmates find their work useful. While more than one-fourth of the inmates do not find their work useful. Although this

TABLE 6.06

Showing the response of the inmates to the question, "Do you find the job which you are doing useful ?"

	Not useful	Can't say	Useful	Total
Frequency	81	24	189	294
Percentage	27.6	8.2	64.3	100

positive response pattern is quite encouraging for this dimension. Even then, given these parameters it becomes partly understandable as to why about 28% of the inmates regard their work only as a means to pass time.

An attempt may be made to ascertain the linkage of different factors with the above opinion pattern. Some of the personal attributes like age (tau= —0.14213; $p<.0001$), caste (tau= 0.05026; $p<.0986$) and the education (tau= .12214; $p<.0009$) of the inmates show significant association in this regard. Among offence-related variables, only term served by the inmates in jail found to be significant ($p<.0008$). As regards the work-related variables is concerned, their present work assignment, however, shows significantly inverse differences (tau= —0.39232; $p<.0001$). Apart from this, liking of job also shows highly significant relationship with this dimension (tau= .36392; $p<.0001$). It is not without interest to look into the reasons as to why the inmates who are doing a different job in the jail do not find it useful. More than three-fourths of them have not provided information; the opinion of the rest is displayed in Table 6.07. The majority of the inmates finds the work irrelevant to the occupational pattern outside in the community. Quite a few also lay emphasise on the unremunerative aspects of work.

TABLE 6.07

Response of the inmates to the question, "If the present job is not useful, what is the reason ?"

	Irrelevant to outside occupational pattern	Different traditional occupation	Nothing in particular	Total
Frequency	58	21	02	81
Percentage	71.6	25.9	2.5	100

None of the personal factors of the inmates show any significant association in this regard. While among the offence-related variables, term of sentence (tau=—0.18428; $p<.0068$) and term served by the inmates in jail (tau= -0.09785; $p<.0950$) show a significant relationship with the inmate opinion outlined above, is negative. The position of work-related variables is, however, the same. To elaborate, the present work assignment of the inmates shows highly significant differences (tau=.23164; $p<.0044$). Interestingly, the opinion of the inmates engaged in different vocational trades (N=192) significantly varies ($p<.0963$) with this. The foregoing data and analysis abundantly bring out that the acquisition of skills is far below the expectation. Nevertheless, it also reveals the circumstances and certain attitudinal positions hampering it.

Achievement level : Towards exploring the above dimension further, the achievement level of the inmates in their respective work/trade has been ascertained. Before proceeding further, it may be restated that like skill development, achievement level depends, from the standpoint of the inmates, on a number of internal and external factors. Above all, it depends on the specific organisational ethos and efforts of the correctional institution. These would be doubtlessly reflected in the approach and the attitude of the officials. Earlier, the view of the officials with regard to the underlying purpose behind the work given to the inmates has been referred to. Whatever the purpose, is it realised ? The trend of the data reflected in Table 6.08 is generally in the affirmative. About 67.5% of the officials

TABLE 6.08

Showing the response of the officials to the question, "Do you feel that present work in Karkhana/Unit achieve the above (desired) purposes ?"

	Not much	Difficult to say	Certainly	Total
Frequency	19	20	81	120
Percentage	15.8	16.7	67.5	100

are categorical in this regard. Nonetheless, this trend may not be accepted without reservations. The opinion of the officials and their educational status are significantly related (tau= .28208; $p < .0001$). Perhaps, the officials who are better educated are also more sceptical about the realisation of the desired objectives behind work. At the same time, the fact may not be lost sight of that most of the officials go by non-reformatory objectives of work and may be expressing opinion only from that wantage point.

Some idea about the achievement level of the inmates in different trades is possible to form should the quality and saleability of goods turned out by the factory sheds are looked into. In this connection, the opinion of the nine vocational instructors was elicited. In respect of the quality of the goods produced by the inmates, they hold a divergent opinion : three of them described the goods as of medium quality while another six of them, of high quality. Evidently, in the matter of production in different factory sheds, there is much scope for improvement and excellence. As regards the saleability of the produce, eight of them hold similar opinion—it is sold fastly. The saleability of goods may not, however, be wholly relied upon as an indicator of the achievement level of the inmates, as the sale of jail produce is prompted by several other extraneous reasons outlined earlier.

Nonetheless, apart from the above mentioned indirect ways adopted to assess the achievement level, a direct method has also been attempted. In order to secure an estimate of the achievement level of the inmates, a ten-point continuum carrying the following instructions has been given to the vocational instructors separately for each inmate :

"The achievement level in the trades in the institutions may be represented on a ten-point scale on which an untrained, unskilled and fresh inmate is represented by zero; and on the other hand, an inmate who is fully trained and possibily as skilled in the trade as the instructor himself, by the numeral ten. Then—

I I I I I I I I I I I

0 1 2 3 4 5 6 7 8 9 10

(i) where would you place this inmate at the time of his entry; and
(ii) where would you place him now ?"

The opinion of the instructors and concerned Headwarder (in case of agriculture, kitchen etc.) was collected. Further, an assessment also of those inmates was secured who were only recently transferred out from the vocational trade. Taken together, information has been gathered in respect of 181 inmates. For the purposes of analysis they have been grouped into :

(a) Low achievers; scores between 0 and 2;
(b) Medium achievers; scores between 3 and 6;
(c) High achievers; score above 6.

The distribution, thus, obtained is presented in Table 6.09. While 85.5% of the inmates have been rated as medium achievers, and 10.7% of them, as high achievers. Nonetheless, only 3.9% of the inmates are low achievers represent as slight personal failure of the inmates as of the instructional organisation and procedures directed at their skill development. The latter contention draws further strength from subsequent analysis.

Several personal attributes of the inmates like age, religion, caste, physical fitness and vice-level have been examined in relation to their achievement level. None of them was found to be significant except only educational status of the inmates shows a good deal of relationship with the achievement level (tau= .08210; $p<.0120$). This clearly indicated that achievement in vocational trades is unrelated to personal factors except educational status of the inmates. In contrast, many offence related variables were found to be important. Although, the offence for which the inmates had been convicted did not show any significant variation with achievement level of the inmate, while, it would be recalled, in quite a few situations the time syndrome had shown significant variation. So is the case here. The term of sentence (tau=0.05279; $p<.0734$) and term served (tau=.09470; $p<.0046$) show a highly significant difference (the probability value of chi-square distribution is 0.004 or less in both cases); related to achievement level. Obviously, the

TABLE 6.09

Educational status of the inmates, their achievement level and term served by them,

Education	Achievement level	Term served (in months) —6	7—12	13—24	25+	Total
	Low	—	01	06	01	08
Illiterate	Medium	04	09	21	55	89
	High	—	—	03	04	07
	Low	—	—	—	—	00
Primary	Medium	—	02	09	25	36
	High	—	—	—	02	02
	Low	—	—	—	—	00
Secondary	Medium	01	03	02	09	15
	High	—	—	—	—	00
	Low	—	—	04	—	04
High School	Medium	01	01	—	15	17
& above	High	—	—	—	03	03
Total		06	16	45	114	181

inmates who were in the jail longer were able to pickup more skills. However, the possibility may be kept in view that long termers, for several intrinsic reasons, may have greater interest and involvement in work. On the above view-point, the institution under study has a encouraging achievement level of the inmates, because of, the majority of long termers.

As would be expected, a large number of work—related variables are found important in relation to achievement level of the inmates. The understanding of underlying purpose behind work shows a significant difference ($p<.0194$). The inmates who mention reformatory objectives ("to learn same skill". and "to do a job after release") are rated better than others. The variable 'Purpose behind work' may be assumed ordinal. Given this assumption, there is seen a high degree of correlation between purpose behind work and the achievement level of the inmates (tau=.15698; $p<.0001$). From this stems the interpretation that the inmates who are aware and perhaps give priority to reformatory objectives of work programmes, are high achievers. Nevertheless, the intervening influence of the term served and the educational status of the inmates may well be kept in view while interpreting the relationship between the achievement level and purpose behind work. On going through this analysis, it would be concluded that in skill development or in achievement of skills and understanding as also awareness of the underlying purpose behind work is one of the most important factors. The inference calls for a conscious efforts to orient the officials as well as the inmates into the reformatory objectives of work programmes.

Next, attention may be diverted to other work-related variables. Present work assignment of the inmates has a significant bearing on the level of achievement ($p<.0001$). Marginally, the inmates in vocational trades are better achievers than others. Likewise, the perception of the inmates of the impartiality in assignment or in tasks in the work sheds, adequacy of the equipment and the quality of raw material—all show mild to sizable variations in this regard. Notable, however, is the linkage between appreciation and praise received by them and their achievement level (tau=.05514; $p<0.0648$). Apparently, the inmates whose efforts and work are appreciated and recognised are better achievers, or, conversely, achievers are appreciated more than others. A similar interrelation is observed in respect of the usefulness or the utility of the work as perceived by the inmates ($p<.0091$). It follows that the inmates who view their work as useful are better achievers and vice-versa. This dimension merits a closer scrutiny.

The level of achievement of the inmates has been examined in relation to the liking they have for their work in the jail. These two variables show a strong relationship with each other (tau=.04857; $p<.0910$). It may be inferred that the inmates who like their work score higher on the achievement scale. This is also supported by common observation. Thus, it would be justifiable to conclude that liking for work is closely (casually ?) related to the level of achievement.

While on this, liked or disliked features of the job which the inmates are doing may be focalised. It is observed that most attractive features of the job ($p<.0019$) mentioned by the inmates as a high achievers has a good deal of relationship with the level of achievement ($tau=.06630$; $p<.0370$) on the one hand and the inmates who mention unsatisfying assignment as the most disliked features of job shows a significant variation as under-achievers ($p<.0002$) with the level of achievement on the other hand. Apparently, job preference and the achievement level are a good deal interdependent.

Yet another variable which needs some attention is willingness/unwillingness of the inmates to switch their present work-assignment. The crosstabulation of the two variables shows a highly significant association ($p<.0011$) with the level of the achievement.

As would have been adduced, formal education of the inmates has only a negligible influence on their achievement level. This line of contention has been persued further (see Table 6.09). It is seen that the educated inmates are only marginally better achievers; and education beyond primary level (5%) is not much relevant to the work in the jail and thereby to the achievement level. Besides, the amount of time spent in the jail is important more than the educational status insofar as the achievement level is concerned.

The analysis of the level of achievement of the inmates in the vocational trade assigned to them in the jail, once again, brings out importance of the work-related variables over offence-related and personal variables.

REHABILITATIVE OUTLOOK

While the rehabilitative value of treatment programmes including work programmes has been emphasized, there is a sizable section comprising both academicians and practitioners who are sceptical about it. Prisons prison programmes, argues

Murton (1976) hardly improve, they are orbital in nature. To what extent do they reform and rehabilitate offenders, or do they do it at all—are the issues which are far from being settled. Likewise, the premise that the offenders who satisfactorily partake of work get successfully reinserted into society, is also disputed. Is rehabilitation dead (Carney, 1980) ?

The situational reality, however, needs to be kept in view. Correctional services represents a people-changing activity which calls for more than routine work at all the levels of the concerned organisations. Given specific organisational interest in and commitment of the staff to treatment, correctional services may have the capacity to achieve what they are supposed to achieve. Similarly, if work programmes may develop the rehabilitative value of the kind as visualised by Sutherland (1968), if they are properly planned and implemented. Nijboer (1971) observes that the successful completion of *systematic* training programmes leads to the continuity of employment in the post-release period, in a significant number of cases. Concerning a few special projects in the United States, Hodgkin (1972) reports that in the post-release period nearly three-fourths of the inmates were having steady jobs. All things considered, the issue of rehabilitation and post-release employment needs further exploration.

This theme is also relevant towards assessing the impact of work programmes on inmates. Nevertheless, this dimension requires postrelease investigation—which is not within the scope of the present study. However, some assessment is possible to make by ascertaining the viewpoint of the officials and the inmates.

Viewpoint of the officials : It can hardly be argued that the rehabilitational potential of work programmes builds up over entire period the inmates remains in the institution. Organisational approach, priorities and procedures, on the one hand, and an inmate's background, his understanding of the purposes and the quality of his participation in work, on the other, all have a critical and contributory role. It would be recalled that many of these dimensions have been subjected to analysis earlier. For the present, an attempt has been made to ascertain the viewpoint of the staff whether inmates need work programmes for their rehabilitation (Table 6.10). Except for a few officials, most of them recognized the rehabilitative value of work. In fact, nearly 27% of them were emphatic about it. This response-pattern assumes a pointed significance in view of the fact that it was closely related to the educational level of the officials ($tau=.14669$; $p<.0085$). The officials who were better educated felt more strongly about the rehabilitative value of work programmes. Still stronger correlation is seen when this dimension is examined in relation to correctional orientation of the officials ($tau=.2575$; $p<.0015$). This suggests that the officials who gave priority to their correctional role, see much rehabilitative value in work programmes.

TABLE 6.10

Response of the officials to the question, "Do you feel that inmates need these work programmes for their rehabilitation ?"

	No	Can't say	To some extent	Definitely	Total	NA
Frequency	01	03	83	32	120	1
Percentage	0.8	2.5	69.7	26.9	100	(0.8)

At this stage, it may be pointed out that the jail has no system of follow-up. Also, it does not maintain any record which would show who is doing what in the post-release period. However, the opinion of the vocational instructors on the subject may be of some relevance. Do the inmates continue with the trade they learn in the jail ? The five instructors out of nine were positive in this regard. While the other four instructors were not sure about it. Has any inmate continued the trade, after release ? How many ? While two instructors were of the opinion that most of the inmates did so, the other seven gave a guarded reply, "Some of the inmates do so". On the whole, the capacity of work programmes to bring about an effective economic readjustment of the inmates after their release is recognised by the jail officials, it is not much clear as to what extent this has actually come about.

View point of the inmates : In the preceding sections, aspects like attractiveness and relevance of the work or trade the inmates are doing, have been highlighted. To a good deal, they also hint at their rehabilitational potential. Notwithstanding this, an attempt has been made to get at the intention of the inmates about pursuing the job they are doing in the jail (Table 6.11). More than three-fourths of the inmates are straightforward in expressing their opinion. They do not intend to continue doing the job/trade which they are doing, after their release. Certainly, this response pattern is discouraging. Nonetheless, the reasons for this are not very complicated. Many of them have been referred to earlier and some of them would delineated a little later.

Caste of the inmates appears to have implications for the response pattern reflected in Table 6.11. For example, 13.1%

TABLE 6.11

Responses of the inmates to the question, "Do you intend to continue of this job/trade after you are released ?

	No	Can't say	Yes	Total
Frequency	260	05	72	337
Percentage	77.2	1.5	21.4	100

of the Brahmin inmates did not intend to continue with the trade ($p<.0323$). That caste has occupational underpinnings and that no deliberate attempt is made in the jail to match work with inmate background, is evident, here. On the other hand, the term of sentence ($tau=.06797$; $p<.0309$) and amount of time spent in the jail appears to have a positive influence ($tau=.15908$; $p<.0001$) on the intention of the inmates to continue the trade. Perhaps, the inmates who were in the jail longer found it easier to continue with the trade than to rebuild old or different economic pursuits.

A large number of work-related variables are significant in this respect. In this connection, a mention may be made of the understanding of the reformatory objectives, liking for the present assignment has a good deal of relationship (tau=.10755; $p<.0016$) with this issue. The level of achievement is also found significantly linked with the kind of intention (tau=.15698; $p<.0001$). While on this, attention may be paid to the present work assignment of the inmates. This shows significant but inverse variation with the intention of the inmates (tau=—0.10729; $p<.0027$). As would be expected, a sizable section of the inmates in vocational trades (57%) intend to persue what they are doing; and in respect of the rest, the data trend is, taken together, unclear. A focused attention, however, needs to be paid to inter-trade differences ($p<.0001$). The highest proportion of the inmates who wish to continue with the trade after-release is in farming (63.5%) and the lowest is oil-press machine (38%). From the rehabilitative angle, the trade preference, in descending order, is : agriculture (63.5%), weaving (11.5%), power-loom (7.7%), spinning (7.7%), tailoring (5.8%), and oil-press machine (3.8%). This data angle, among other things, is much thought-provoking as to the relevance of various trades made available to the inmates in the jail.

This line of analysis has been persued and an attempt has been made to find out the difficulties the inmates foresee in continuing the trade in the post-release period (Table 6.12). Less than one-fourth of the inmates did not expressed their opinion on the subject. Among the remaining, a vast majority (95.4%) of the inmates refered to their family occupation being different from what they were doing in the jail. For some, to establish necessary capital for investment to start a trade was a hurdle. Only one inmate mentioned the social stigma he was likely to carry for being a convict in jail.

This data distribution apart, it is doubtful that these and similar consideration ever go into the planning and organisation of work for the inmates in the jail.

Quite a few family and offence-related variables show significant variation with the above responses of the inmates. By passing these, attention may be diverted to work related

TABLE 6.12

Responses of the inmates to the question, "Would you continue the trade after-release, what are the difficulties you foresee in doing so ?"

	Family occupation different	Not relevant/ paying	Finance/ capital	Stigma because jailed	Total
Frequency	249	07	04	01	261
Percentage	95.4	2.7	1.5	0.4	100

variables. The liking for the job which the inmates are doing, does not appears to be statistically important (the data are too skewed for chi-square distribution). In accordance with the number of jobs assigned in jail, highly significant differences are observed (tau=0.13548; $p<.0005$). Besides this, purpose behind work also has a good deal of relationship with this ($p<.0088$). In terms of vocational trades, this has a significant linkage with the issue ($p<.0202$). Relatively speaking, most of the inmates in vocational trade (63.8%) and inmate service (15.3%) refer to family occupation being different, and those in maintenance (21%) mention their work/trade as being not paying. Finally, it may be remarked that the overwhelming majority of the officials stresses on the rehabilitative value of work in the jail. The vocational instructors were rather emphatic that after their release most of the inmates continued the trade. In sharp contrast, the bulk of the inmates had no intention of doing so. Perhaps, work-programmes and related procedures need to be further streamlined so that their potential is fully exploited.

While looking into the impact of work programmes on the inmates in the jail under study, the influence of personal, offence-related and work-related variables has been evaluated. In the assessment of the inmates themselves a vast majority of theirs was given to lethargy. The position is not, however, so much discouraging when their sense of vocational efficacy, work satisfaction and team work are examined. It may be noted that few personal factors are important in this regard. In contrast, a few offence-related and a large number of work-related variables show significant association. Role adherence by the inmates has also been studied. The opinion of the officials with regard to change in behaviour of those inmates who satisfactorily participate in work is more or less divided. On the specific issue, of inmates conducting themselves to the satisfaction of the officials, the opinion of the latter is a shade better than of the former. Contrariwise, on the issues such as reformation and selfless working of the inmates, the opinion of the inmates trails behind that of the officials. As far as the opinion of the inmates is concerned, the notable influencing forces are offence-related and work-related variables.

Very few officials were of the opinion that the inmates were earnest about work. However, this may well be examined in relation to several limiting conditions. This apart, a very few of the inmates reported that they had learned any new work skill. Likewise, less than three-fourths (65%) of them found their work as relevant or useful. For this, they also gave cogent reasons. All along, the opinion of the inmates was seen to correspond with work-related variables, and, to some extent, with offence-related variables.

The purpose underlying work is understood by the officials. Atleast, more than half (67.5%) of them were emphatic about it. Similarly, the vocational instructors were eloquent about the saleability of the goods produced in the factory sheds. These parameters do provide a general idea of the achievement level of the inmates in work; but it may not be wholly dependable.

Achievement in different work/trades has been assessed with the help of vocational instructors and others. Nearly eleven per cent of the inmates are rated as high achievers as against 3.9% low achievers. Extensive analysis has been carried out to evaluate the significance of different sets of variables. Nevertheless, the results are little different from those obtained earlier:

to some extent, offence-related variables, and, to a large extent, work-related variables have a determining influence on the achievement level. It may be reiterated that few personal variables have shown a significant linkage. In view of the notion that illiteracy among the inmates is a major stumbling block in work-programmes, the educational status of the inmates has been scrutinised from many different angles. However, the educational status of the inmates is seen in no way a factor in their acquisition of work skills or achievement level.

Most officials stood by the rehabilitative value of work. In juxtaposition, a small section of the inmates showed a disinclination towards continuing with the trade learnt in the jail after their release. They offered several plausible reasons for this. Not many independent variables were relevant in this respect—if at all, they were work-related variables. The data and their analysis fully substantiate the hypothesis under examination.

7

Conclusion

If criminal justice development in the country has faced a relative neglect, it is more so true with corrections, in general, and jails, in particular (Khan and Chilad, 1982). Overcrowding, unsatisfactory living conditions and indifferent correctional programmes are some of the inadequacies which have been, time and again, underlined. This apart, a few generic issues also need to be focalised.

In contemporary times, correctional institutions are expected to exert therapeutic influence on those persons who come in conflict with law and to reintegrate them into society. The nature and magnitude of this task demands a modicum of purposiveness, a coordinated organisational approach and a concerted effort by all concerned (Khan, 1981). Have these been forthcoming ? More often than not, citizens are interested in little more than offloading their bothersome brethern into jail so as to maintain the stance of virtuosity (Konopka, 1974), criminal justice agencies in pushing them behind bars so as to reinforce the letter of law, correctional functionaries in somehow processing them out through the apparatus so as to keep the system going (Reasons and Kaplan, 1975), and the inmates themselves in marking time with a somewhat passive resignation so as to rejoin the community, for good or bad. Taken together, the system appears to be caught between disparate expectations (see also, Kirkpatrick, 1974).

It is thus hardly surprising that the institutional correction, of late, has come in for much criticism. Jails are expensive places to build and run (Zeigler, 1974). They are based on assumptions which are unethical, as coercion and abridgement of human rights are inherent. They do not reform (Bold, 1952) and tend more to be 'houses of darkness' (Orland, 1975) than rehabilitation centres (Carney, 1980). Demoralising, demeaning and dehumanising, the process of prisonisation affects the residents and the officials alike (see, for example, Schmidt, 1971; Haney, et al., 1973). Work programmes and the use of the manpower of the inmates represent a compromise between society's preference in handling antisocial or antilegal behaviour, the jail officials' inclination to use them as a correctional tool; and Singer (1973) observes that the neither objectives is achieved.

Part or much of the criticism levelled against the institutional correction may be justifiable. The difference between the concept and practice, however, may well be kept in view. Is their something wrong in the programme-conceptualisation or in the programme-implementation ? This consideration is more so pertinent in relation to a system on which diverse ideas and practices have been superimposed without paying adequate attention to structural changes and which is, relatively speaking, a victim of societal and official indifference (Khan and Chilad, 1982). Moreover, in regard to correctional institution it is relatively easier to be emotional and critical, and difficult to dispassionately appraise respectives roles of society, government, jails and inmates in their social reclamation.

The present study has attempted to enquire into only one of the many correctional services offered by an institution, namely, work programmes. Towards this, attention has been focused on a big-sized correctional institution, so called the Model Prison in North India. To a considerable extent, the sampled jail may be representative of the institutional correction in the country. Information for the study has been collected from a diverse range of sources: functionaries (N=120) and the inmates (N=337) have been interviewed; the progress of a large number of new entrants to the jail has been followed; the jail routine has been closely observed; and a body of official information has been collected. On the whole, the data thus collected provide an assessment of institutional setting, the inmate community, correctional functionaries, and the form and quality of the work programmes in the institution. As to what extent work by jail inmates as a part of the correctional programmes is able to yield desired results, may be evaluated keeping in view a large perspective.

II

In order to develop and improve a dependable insight into the institutional setting, the jail under study has been appraised in its totality. As such, both formal and informal structures have been looked into with a view to ascertaining jail conditions conducive to the furtherence of correctional objectives.

The institution is not as much overcrowded as is seen in many other central and district jails. The number of residents in the jail (N=355) is only marginally more than its authorised capacity (N=343). This is mainly due to the lack of remand, undertrials and short termers (see Table 2.01). The staffing organisation reflects a definite bias for custodial functions, in that not only are bulk of the functionaries custodial but also the functional status of the treatment staff is definitely low. In terms of financial outlay the institution is barely well off. Over the years, there have been budgetary increases; but they have been hardly large enough to encourage any expansion or development and improvement. Furthermore, if inflationary trends are taken into account, resources provided to the institution are somewhat shrinking.

As far as the custodial functions are concerned, jail procedures appears to be adequate and effective. All the formalities relating to the admission of convicts, their safe-custody in barracks of the Bhawans and the like are being, even ritualistically, observed. Reservations, however, inevitably surface when attention is turned to treatment aspects. The classification of the inmates is although very advanced but more on paper than in reality. General education programmes for the inmates is given, at best, a low priority in the organisational scheme. Since the participation in these is left to the willingness of the inmates, barely six percent of the inmates attend the jail school regularly or intermittently. The jail does spend some money on the recreation of the residents both for indoor and outdoor games. Some game material is also available; but it is used less by the inmates and more by others. Consequently, it is observed that only 17.5% of the inmates participates in games and sports in the institution. Of late, self-reliance among the inmates has been sought to be stimulated through self-government. Towards this end, Prisoners' Panchayats have been conceived. The jail under study does have a similar body; but it is more on office records than in practice. In order to enable the inmates to maintain links with the community outside, they are allowed a certain specified number of interviews or meetings with friends and relatives. Nevertheless, the physical arrangements and official procedures for this are pathetic, crude and far from being agreeable. To encourage the inmates to put up satisfactory conduct and behaviour, they are allowed remissions or 'good days' in their sentence in accordance with laid down rules. The operation of the remission-scheme is, however, highly mechanical. It is debatable whether the seheme is operated skillfully or is able to realise its intrinsic objectives. Although a negative incentive, punishment is important in modifying the inmate behaviour. Some inmates have been punished but mostly on account of disciplinary problems. It is doubtful that it has been consciously used to channelise individual and group behaviour in the desired direction. It goes without saying that the jail routine is highly regimented. Armed guards, custodial staff and convict officers keep vigil round the clock and heads are counted, repeatedly. Perhaps the emphasis on security aspects is far in excess to the genuine requirements of the institution; and that this may be overshadowing treatment functions of the institution is difficult to ruled out (especially in Jamuna Bhawan). Formally speaking, the jail is expected to be visited by certain notified officials and non-officials. They enjoy an advisory capacity.

A description of the jail community would hardly be complete without a reference to informal aspects including informal structures and norms of behaviour. Moreover, informal structures are not particular to inmates alone—they encompass staff as well. It is observed that in the jail, after the Superintendent, Deputy Superintendent and Jailor, the position of the Octagon Officer (Deputy Jailor in rank) is very important, because he does the time-keeping of the inmates. The jail administration heavily relies on Convict Officers (nearly 13%). At the cutting-edge level, they share administrative chores in a substantial manner. Treatment functionaries have only a secondary place and relatively a lower prestige in the jail. Training instructors and the teacher having the status equivalent only to a head-warder play even a more subdued role.

As mentioned earlier, there is inadequate classification system in the jail. A new entrant spends several days almost aimlessly before he is assigned to a work unit, perhaps short in manpower. Apart from formal mode of punishment, a few informal means are also adopted to discipline and erring and recalcitrant inmates : and these means may not necessarily conform to law or rules (see, also Greenberg and Stander, 1972).

Inmates in the jail have their own set of norms and values. Though not a too enviable predicament, many of them are caste-conscious. All of them nurse a sense of injury against society as well as against criminal justice. They face adjustment problems in the jail community. Many among them (60%) are viewed with suspicion by the fellow inmates for passing information on the goings-on in the jail community to the officials. Some of them (34.1%) are also looked down upon as the favourites (stooges ?) of the jail high-ups. This kind of lack of mutual trust or abundance of hostility becomes more so apparent in respect of Convict Officers. Most Convict-Warders, Convict-Overseers and Night Watchmen are disliked for their overbearing manners and dealings. Even otherwise, many Convict Officers, reportedly, are not above board. Some of them take a cut from the gifts received by the inmates during the course of their interview or meeting with friends and relatives. What is more, quite a few inmates run into conflict with Convict Officers, of course, with unpleasant consequences. Among the inmates, gossip is a popular pastime. They talk about food, jail officials, Convict Overseers and the like. Interestingly, the jail has quite a flourishing underground economy. Though illegal, many inmates carry cash on their person. On the other hand, eatables, groceries, *bidis* and other drugs are clandestinely traded against cash or kind. Several information-sources converge on the existence of the problem of homosexuality amongst the residents. In the absence of a system of conjugal visits, the problem is not wholly unexpected.

In spite of the adverse circumstances and the effect of prisonisation, inmates have not become devoid of lofty values. Many of them regularly observe religious rites, help fellow inmates and share joys and sorrows. Taken together, the jail appears to have almost all the strengths and failings of the human groups beyond the walls. This apart, its formal organisation as an apparatus meant for the social reclamation of the digressed leaves much to be desired.

While discussing a correctional measure like work programmes, attention has to be focused on the basic material, namely, the inmates. Whether work programmes are an instrument of change or a source of diversion, would depend much on the background of the inmates and their capacity for work and training. In the same direction, personal characteristics of the inmates are a major determinant of adjustment between them and the jail environment, as also of their receptivity of various therapeutic services including work programmes. It is observed that most of them are about 28 years in age, about 81 percent of them are Hindus, more than half (52.2%) of them belong to lower caste groups and 52.5% of them are literate. It is worth mentioning that most of the inmates prior to their being convicted were leading a settled life : more than three-fourths (77.7%) of them are married. What is more, a vast majority of the inmates are not given to addictive drugs like tobacco, cannabis and alcohol. Hence, it shows a majority of them have a low vice-level. While more than one-fourth of them (28.8%) are completely non-users of drug. All things considered, personal characteristics of the inmates are not very promising in so far as vocational training is concerned. Much, however, would depend upon the areas, forms and the quality of vocational training and work. Are the existing vocational training programmes really very demanding ?

What is the nature of the family the inmates come from ? The single family system appears to survive, atleast, in relation to the inmates, and more than three-fourths (76.2%) of them come from single families. Indeed, theirs are large family groups (average number of members in the household, 5.09). The general literacy level of these inmate families appears to be equal than that of the inmate themselves (60% in each case). Much of this difference could be explained in terms of the behavioural background of the inmates. That they come from lower economic strata is borned out by the data. Most of them (89%) come from agricultural families. The household income is also modest. As far as the family background of the inmates is concerned there is nothing encouraging vis-a-vis work programmes; but there is seen nothing discouraging either.

Most of the inmates (81.3%) have been involved in murder, followed by those, for dacoity (14.2%). Among them, a vast majority (99.4%) of them are first offenders. Yet another feature worth noting is that three-fourths of them have violated law in group. It follows that almost all of them are undergoing long term of imprisonment i.e. more than six years. Viewed from a criminological angle, crime and sentence of the inmates is somewhat disquieting; but looked at from the correctional angle, it is not as bad-the bulk of them cannot be termed as hardened criminals. Since a majority of them have been involved in group offences, they may not be an altogether anti-social lot. Furthermore, the institution has an opportunity to plan and exert therapeutic influence on them as they would be with it for longer periods of time.

Several other encouraging inmate characteristics come to

light when their self-reported role norms are looked into. Mutual help, camaraderie and so forth are found in the inmates in a good and sufficient measure. There are a few limiting conditions as well. Many of them are given to casteism and interpersonal conflict. Nevertbeless, most of them have a healthy outlook towards life and future.

On all the counts—their personal characteristics, family background crime and sentence and role norms—it is not easy to assert that the inmates are clearly suited to vocational training or work. Nonetheless, this issue needs to be examined in relation to the technical complexity of the work programmes currently operational in the jail. Moreover, the situational position may not be lost sight of that the inmates are not there to learn, they are there to be taught sufficiently.

If the background and capacity of the inmates are important for the success of the prison process, equally important are the jail functionaries. Reformatory ideals and the correctional policy would remain a cliche-ridden abstraction, if the officials at the cutting-edge level do not have the requisite aptitude, orientation, professional background and a gift of human understanding and empathy. In the jail under study, the officials are middle-aged (average age of 45 years) and modestly educated (26% are educated upto graduation and post-graduation). It may not be of much consequence that 88.3% of them are Hindus. What is, however, notable is that 71 per cent of them are from upper caste groups. This stands in sharp contrast with the caste of the inmates in the jail (about 20 per cent of them belong to lower caste groups). Professional background of the jail functionaries does not inspire much confidence. A vast majority (97.5%) of them had no job-experience at the time of joining the jail service. What is more, more than three-fourths (88.3%) of them have not undergone any professional training. Whatever they have by way of training is on the job training which is, indeed, considerable, quantitatively (average length of service, 15 years). Nevertheless, the point relating to job-experience may well not be stretched beyond a point, because unduly long durations often result in an archetyped approach in working, and resist new ideas. Earlier, a reference to custodial and treatment staff has been made showing that treatment functionaries are fewer and have low functional status.

Some attention has also been paid to the 'staff-culture', obtaining in the jail. Communication channels between the jail functionaries are not very fluent. An interchange of ideas on professional and operational problems between the colleagues of the same rank is, at best, occasional and restrictive. It is more so restrictive when it comes to interaction between subordinates and Superordinates. Perhaps, superior officers in the jail are much given to bureaucratic and hierarchical working. Seldom do they consult subordinates while ordering alterations cutting across their functional areas, only occasionally listen to their problems, or try to solve them. Likewise, rarely do the superiors have a word of praise for the subordinates and their efforts. It follows that few jail functionaries venture to disagree even on professional matters with their superiors. These informal aspects, on the whole, hardly augur well for a welfare service organisation like jail.

What are the role models the jail functionaries have before them ? In their opinion, the least successful officer is one who is strict, generally lazy, uncooperative with colleagues, corrupt, and inefficient in his working. Conversely, the most successful jail officer, in their view, is one who, in the descending order, is knowledgeable, concerned with the welfare of the inmates, efficient, bold, honest, and concerned with the jail-machinery. Perhaps, probity is important in jail but it does not merit priority.

Whether in welfare services or correctional services, functionaries cannot subsist on zeal alone. If they are to give their best to the service, they have to have a measure of job satisfaction. In the jail under study, the level of job-satisfaction has not been found to be very satisfactory. In this direction, attention has been paid to several determinants of job-satisfaction. About 68 per cent of the officials have had no promotion. Small wonder that many of them are given to cynicism in respect of promotions and promotion criteria. To illustrate the point, the majority of the officials do not think that educational level has a bearing on promotion chances and many of them mention intervention from the influential and the opinion of the superiors as being helpful in securing promotions. This apart, most of them like their present job. To great extent, job aspects like security of service, appreciation by superiors, cooperation from colleagues, easy nature of work, and prestige in society appeal to them. In contrast, they appear to be unhappy about the salary structure, promotion avenues and the working conditions they have in the jail. A majority of them find their job as pleasant and a little useful but at all boring, and about 72% of them are willing to switch their job if an equivalent career were available. It falls into pattern that 95% of them do not wish their son to join the jail service.

Although the level of job satisfaction in the functionaries is generally medium, they, it is refreshing to note, identify their role. To exemplify, a vast majority (about 99 per cent) are aware of their role norms. The inmates also think that the jail officials are generally helpful to them. However, this line of contention is also kept up when the role adherence on the part of the officials is enquired into. Do they help and guide the inmates and generally function to the satisfaction of the clientele—on all these issues their own responses are encouraging; and this is further reinforced by the opinion of the inmates. That their working is overtly concerned with the custodial functions or the security aspects of the jail, is brought out by their own response pattern as well as that of the inmates. What is more disconcerting, most staff members somewhat resent interaction with the inmates. As a matter of fact their role perception on the whole is somewhat distorted. Team work, fuller participation in correctional programmes and similar issues evoke only divided opinion. Apparently, there is much scope to reorient the staff to the correctional philosophy and practice.

Yet another important consideration in the success of work programmes and hence institutional correction is the sufficiency of work programmes themselves, To what extent they would be able to bring about a change in the behaviour of the inmates and equip them to get rehabilitated in the postrelease period, would largely depend on their being purposive and inmate-oriented. It may be reiterated that the inmates in the institution under study are divided into three broad groups : Vocational training, Inmate Service, and Maintenance. A closer look at different work units like agriculture, power-loom, paper-making, weaving unit and jail kitchen brings out quite a few organisational features of work programmes which are not adequately encouraging. Mechanisation and general working conditions have been given insufficient attention. As a matter of fact in most work units, inmates work to learn and not learn to work. This contention is further reinforced by the fact that conscious and formal methods are seldom employed to impart skills. Besides, the issue of relating work programmes to the outside labour-market demands becomes more pertinent. Work in the maintenance-unit as well as inmate service is largely irrelevant. Except for agriculture, the relevance of other vocational trades is partially or wholly doubtful. The indifferent nature of purposiveness in the work organised in the institution is further reflected in the distribution of the inmates over different work units. About 64 per cent of them are assigned to vocational trades; 15 per cent in inmate service; 21 per cent in maintenance work and 11% of them are working as convict officers. This kind of imbalance persists in the distribution of the inmates over different vocational trades. To illustrate the point, 20.3% of them are deployed in agriculture, the predominent rural-agricultural background of the inmate-population notwithstanding. While 19.3% of them on powerloom and dyeing; 18.2% on weaving; and 17.2% of them are engaged in spinning. This casts serious doubts on the inmate-orientation in the work given to them. The unclarity in approach and assumptions surrounding work by the jail inmates further shows up when, in this regards, the viewpoints of staff as well as of the inmates are ascertained. To the majority of the staff, work is a mere disciplinary measure, and to the majority of the inmates only a means to pass time. Very few in both the groups mention reformatory and rehabilitative aspects of work. This kind of lack of understanding is adversely affecting the organisation and working of work programmes in the jail, in no small way. Usually, the classification system based on a study of the background, personality-needs and aptitude of the inmates would be assumed to be the core mechanism through which they are assigned to different work-units. The data, however, bring, out a position which hardly confirms to this. Barely 6.5% of the inmates had a hand in choosing their work; and the rest of them have been assigned (arbitrarily ?) work by the officials. It is linked with their background ? Apparently, educational status of the inmates has bearing on this, age of the inmates is somewhat important, and their term of sentence along with their offence is a major determinant. Factory-sheds are mostly manned by the long termers, and jail-kitchen by the upper caste Hindus. It is, therefore, observed that the bulk of the inmates (85.2%) are like their work. While a sizable section (14.8%) of them are dislike or indifferent their work. This kind of indifference or dislike is not particular only to the maintenance unit and inmate-service; it is there in respect of certain vocational trades. For example, inmates in oil-press machine, weaving and spinning are dislike their work. In spite of their low educational status and the apathy, which the process of prisonisation invariably generates, they know what they like or do not like in their work. Apart from the arbitrary nature of work assignment, the inmates have been shifted from work unit to work unit, often more than once. Also, quite a few of them are willing to change, perhaps to the trades having a large rehabilitative value.

Attention has also been paid to the infrastructural facilities in the jail. The provision of trained and experienced vocational instructors in different trades is far from being adequate. Likewise, the provision of machines, tools or equipments is somewhat unsatisfactory. There are only two trades (agriculture and powerloom) which have been considerably modernised mechanically but the maintenance of these unit is far from satisfactory. This apart, some amount of mechanisation is also needed in inmate service and the maintenance unit. The maintenance of whatever equipment is available is poor. Although the supply of raw-material is viewed both by the staff and the inmates as satisfactory, it needs to be looked into closely and separately. For the present, it would suffice to state that supply of raw-material is apparently linked neither with the prison policy, jail budget and correctional programmes, nor with the number of inmates in the jail, size of the order-book or turnover of the factory-sheds. At the same time, the goods produced in the factory sheds seldom stockpile. It does not necessarily reflect the quality or the competitiveness of the produce – it owes much to pricing policy of the jail and the purchasing policy of the sister government departments. It may be remarked here that all the sale or purchase of goods produced in the jail, is done by the Jail Depot., Lucknow, in open market.

In relation to work by the jail inmates, motivations available to them have been brought under focus. Both formal or informal means of punishments are reportedly used to affect and modify the inmate-behaviour. Nonetheless, there is little evidence to suggest that the punishment has been systematically used in relation to the performance in factory-sheds. Among different positive incentives, even the word of praise has been used only sparingly. And, of course, the institution have a system of offering wages or comparable wages to the inmates; but does not have any system of awarding certificates or medals. The institution under study, offer wages to inmates for their labour, wages and remission go together. The inmates also feel likewise.

With this backdrop of the institutional setting, inmates' characteristics, staffing pattern and the availability of work programmes in the institution, the impact of the work programmes on the inmates has been assessed by looking into their role identification, achievement of skills, and anticipation of rehabilitative prospects. The inmates have somewhat poor self-esteem, yet they feel important with regard to the work they are doing in the jail, and many of them (94.4%) emphasise team work. Role adherence by the inmates has also been examined—both through the staff and the inmates. This is in the expected direction, in that most of the inmates understandably enough, express a favourable opinion about themselves : they complete their sentence without displeasing jail officials;

they use time in the jail to improve their conduct and behaviour, and they selflessly work and work hard. What is somewhat unexpected is the favourable disposition of the officials towards this. However, they are sceptic about the willing participation of the inmates in work programmes. Most of them attribute their participation to jail rules—indeed, a limiting condition. Is this a considered opinion or a stereotype ?

Have the inmates learnt anything new (if the work assigned corresponds with what they were doing prior to their imprisonment), or useful (if the two are different) ? On either counts the position is not very encouraging—it is not so even in respect of those engaged in vocational trades. This apart, a direct attempt has been made to secure an estimate of the skill-achievement by the inmates. Ascertained with the help of vocational instructors, the achievement level of the inmates is not very discouraging : if 85.5% of the inmates have been rated medium in achievement level and 10.7% of them have been rated high. Nonetheless, only 3.9% of the inmates have been rated low, represent as slight personal failure of the inmates as of the instructional organisation and procedures directed at their skill development. This dimension has been probed from different causative angles. Few personal or offence-related variables are linked with this. What is more, the educational status of the inmates has a good deal of relationship with the achievement level. In sharp contrast, liking for the work, assignment, understanding of the purpose underlying work, unwillingness to switch work and other work-related variables show a direct relationship.

The inference that work-related factors have a critical bearing on the nature and intensity of the impact of work programmes on the inmates. As would be expected, most of the officials are emphatic on the role and significance of work in the post—release rehabilitation of the inmates. Nevertheless, about 22% of the inmates foresee that they would be able after their release to continue the work learnt in the jail. The difficulties which they visualise are not wholly unfounded. It is thus observed that work programmes have been able to make some impact upon the inmates; and, in this, aspects relating to work itself have been unequivocally important.

III

The assumptions on which the present work is based, perhaps, may bear repetition. Punishment as the societal response to bothersome and objectionable behaviour is essential to maintain peace and harmony in society; the degree of civility in different forms of punishment corresponds with the socio-cultural refinement a society has been able to achieve; towards the social reclamation of those who come in conflict with law, a combination of the institutional, noninstitutional and 'hybrid' techniques (attendance centres, community centres etc.) need to be used; if correctional institutions have not achieved a desired success, it is less due to the insufficiency of the philosophy governing them and more due to several structural and functional inadequacies in the practice at the cutting-edge level; despite scathing criticism, in recent years, institutional correction is likely to remain the principal modality to deal with offenders (Morris, 1974); and, different correctional programmes need to be objectively evaluated so that they are further streamlined and rendered efficacious. Keeping this in view and in the light of the data presented in the preceding sections, a few policy issues which emerge may be highlighted. In the country, jails are a 'state' subject. This constitutional position has greatly facilitated organisational flexibility and contributed towards making jails suited to local conditions. But this has also bred heterogeneity (Khan and Chilad, 1982). Often jail organisation and working in different states and union territories widely differ. In order to bring about uniformity and standardisation in institutional correction in the country, the evolution of a national policy on jails in imperative. Such a policy would spell out larger social purposes behind punishment towards which different correctional agencies should move. It would also lay guidelines for the jail system. Whether jails function merely for containment (as 'warehouses for the long-term storage of human refuse'), or for the reformation of the offender, whether the safe-custody of the inmates is their *raison d'etre*, or the treatment and re-education of those entrusted to their custody are their priority, and similar issues would be thrashed out. From this would flow the clarification whether correctional services, in general, and jail services, in particular, are hierarchical and bureaucratic agencies, or professional and welfare organisations. A national correctional policy in consonance with the modern thinking and in keeping with our occasional policy pronouncements in national and international forums is likely to have the ability to providc a viable framework for action for different types of correctional agencies in the country, from the apex to the grass-roots level. Accordingly, most of the sectoral and smaller issues, e.g., personnel policy, personnel composition, living condition in jails, treatment programmes and the like would be taken care of. The cumulative impact of such a policy most likely would not only invigorate jail services but also standardise them through the length and breadth of the country.

Besides, the jail personnel policy calls for a thorough review. Apparently, among the jail officials, professionalism and identification with the job leave much to be desired. Since emoluments of the jail functionaries are unsatisfactory, promotion avenues limited, and working conditions demanding, the level of job-satisfaction among them is unmistakably low. Likewise, recruitment rules and training procedures have not been properly aligned to treatment and welfare functions. These personnel aspects need to be properly specified. While on this, a reference may be made to the personnel mix between the custodial and treatment staff. In the US, treatment staff accounts for the 29 per cent of the total staff strength in the correctional institutions; and, in sharp contrast, this ratio is only 4 per cent in India. What is more, treatment staff have lower functional status. This is amply reflected on their emoluments, promotion chances, authority in the jail working, intra-staff dealings and staff-inmate relations. Doubtless, these ambiguities in the personnel policy can hardly be allowed to drift.

At the institutional level, too, a few policy issues merit attention. Budget provisions for the institutions including 'contingency' which, among other things, includes expenses on the maintenance of the inmates, need to be revised upwards with due attention to the existing economic indices. To link the budget of the jail department including those of the institutions with the rate of inflation, and the budget-head of 'contingency' with the cost of living index, are some of the major policy issues. Incidentally, this would also provide for the policy guidelines along which budget allocations should be distributed over different heads including that of work programmes. Secondly, the institutional policy and procedures governing the classification of the inmates as laid down in jail manuals need to be further crystallised. Formal procedures envisaging the involvement both of the custodial staff and the specialists need to be specified so as to achieve a proper and scientific classification of the inmates and to individualise the correctional impact. As a logical corollary, such procedures would automatically require an assessment of the personality characteristics as well as aptitude of the inmates, and make various correctional services including work programmes increasingly inmate-oriented. Thirdly, a major policy-decision which needs to be sorted out relates to the continuance of the practice of appointing convict-officers in the jail. Indeed, they shoulder several administrative chores, and, hence, a probable strain on the manpower and financial resources of the jail department is avoided but seldom do they form the bridge, as is often made out, between the staff and the inmate community, or generate among the inmates a sense of participation in the administration of the jail. On the other end, they are directly or indirectly responsible for much coercion, exploitation and corruption. Dispensing with this practice would certainly entail additional inputs in terms of manpower, but additional costs thus involved in the long run are likely to more than repay themselves in terms of a qualitative change in the jail life and a fuller realisation of the organisational objectives.

Concerning work programmes, the very first issue which needs to be grappled with relates to the institutional objectives underlying them. Is work there to carry out the fiat of 'rigorous imprisonment' and exact 'hard labour', or else is it a means to reclaim those entrusted to the institutional care ? A somewhat diffused thinking has thus far permeated the apex policy level, and piled up a plethora of problems at the field level. It flows from this that, secondly, the range of available work programmes needs to be substantially augmented. Many vocational trades currently offered in most jails have outlived their relevance and need to be dropped, and many more need to be added, most certainly, in line with the occupational pattern and labour-market demands outside in the community. A sufficiently wide range of carefully selected vocational trades would also enable the matching of the interests and aptitude of the individual inmates. In this regard, it is for consideration that 'agricultural jails' should be organised in every state, perhaps in conjunction with some agriculture college/university. Thirdly, the organisation and management of work programmes may well not be left to traditional and perhaps outdated techniques. They need to be organised with a modern management outlook so that both staff and inmates are able to galvanise their efforts to evolve a truly participative group. Perhaps, a vocational training officer, with appropriate status and authority should be appointed in every jail having a convict population of 200 or thereabout. This measure coupled with proper superior supervision should be able to tackle many problems of training, production and distribution, in a satisfactory manner. Lastly, since official routine and requirements are no substitute for internal motivation, a properly coordinated incentive structure need to be evolved outlining nonmonetary as well as monetary incentives to the inmates engaged in production activities. Based either on a flat rate or a piece-rate, realistic wages need to be paid to the such inmates in view of several philosophical and pragmatic reasons.

IV

The burden of the present study is that work programmes as part of larger correctional services are important to institutional correction everywhere, but they are crucial to a developing country like India. As mentioned earlier, during the preceding decades, through planned economic development, the country has striven to strengthen its agricultural and industrial base—

with considerable success. It would not take long to see that a plea to augment and intensify work programmes in jails is in keeping with this national endeavour, however, small or limited the scale may be.

As the present study shows, institutional correction and hence work by jail inmates have scarcely been given the attention they deserve. It follows that their role in the reclamation of offenders and in crime prevention is not sufficiently appreciated. Concerning work programmes, often reasons for not doing anything are offered more easily than for doing something. More often than not, the background and the capability of the inmate population are held against work programmes, their development, and investments on them. It may be conceded that all the inmates are not teachable. But, are all of them unteachable ? Are the nature and complexity of all the trades such which make heavy demands on the inmates' educational level ? In several quarters, the issue of resource-constraint is raised. It can hardly be gainsaid that, at the present stage of resource development in the country, priorities are many and means limited. Nevertheless, economic development and criminal justice development need to go together. Besides, something is possible to bring about even by diverting and reallocating available resources. For example, 'adult education programme' may very well cover large jails like Model Jail, without any loss of focus or involvement of additional expenditure. Similarly, in almost all the district headquarter towns, in recent years, industrial-technical institute have been organised to develop manpower resources through short-term vocational training programmes. It may not be altogether out of place to suggest that a part of the investment may be diverted to organise similar facilities, to begin with, within or alongside open jails. This apart attention ought to be paid to the staffing pattern in jails. As argued earlier, jails, as at present, lean heavily towards custodial functions and hence in favour of the custodial staff. Among other things, this militates with our intentions and commitment to treatment-orientation. Perhaps, a balance is possible to bring about by allowing a larger investment on work programmes and by having a few intermediate level posts of training instructors/officers.

Vocational training and work by jail inmates need to be given a fair-chance, in terms of organisational priorities, resources and infra-structure. Given these enabling conditions, they are bound to prove their worth, and to dispel much of the existing indifference and scepticism. This appears to be prudent and imperative, for work programmes, the present study brings out, have a large potential of making a positive and significant contribution not only towards a fuller realisation of the organisational objectives but also towards nation-building.

Bibliography

Adams, W.T. et al., (1966) The Relationship of Correctional to Vocational Rehabilitation. *Crime and Delinquency*, 12, 3, 227-31.

Aday, R.H. (1977) Toward the Development of a Therapeutic Programe for Older Prisoners. *Offender Rehabs.*, 1, 4, 343-348.

Alexander, M.E., (1957) *Jail Administration.* Springfield : C. C. Thomas Publishers.

Anastasi, A., (1964) *Fields of Applied Psychology.* New York : McGraw-Hill.

Andry, R.G., (1963) *The Short-term Prisoner.* London : Steven.

Arm Strong, J., (1950) *Incentive and Quality.* London: Chapman & Hall.

Bailey, W., (1966) Correctional Outcome : An Evaluation of 100 Reports. *J. of Criminal Law, Criminology and Police Science*, 5, 153, 155-57.

Banks, F., (1958) *Teach them to live.* New York : Inter-University Press.

Baril, F.W., (1967) Vocational Training in Canadian Penitentiaries. *J. Correct. Educ.*, 19, 2, 16-17, and 27-28.

Barnes, E.H. & Teeters, K.N., (1966) *New Horizons in Criminology.* Englewood Cliffs : Prentice-Hall.

Bernhardt, E. (1969) Work in Penitentiary Institutions—a Means of Social Education ? *Schwabisch Hall.*, Z. Straf Voll 249, 18, 1, 48-52.

Bisno, H., (1952) *The Philosophy of Social Work.* Washington : Public Affairs Publishers.

Bogardus, E.S., (1949) *Sociology*, New York : MacMillan.

Bold, G.B., (1952) Does the Prison Reform ? *The Annals of the American Academy of Political and Social Science*, 284, 42-46.

Brando, S. (1967) The Remuneration of Penitentiary Work in the context of Comparative Law. *Rev. Penit. Penal*, 91, 2, 359-370.

Borckway, Z.R. (1912) *Fifty years of prison service.* New York : Charities Publication.

Brown, B.S., Dupont, R.L., Kozel, N.J. & Spevacek, J.D., (1971) Staff Conception of Inmate Characteristics : a comparison of Treatment and Custodial Staffs at *Criminology*, 9, 2-3, 316-379.

Caird, R., (1972) Prison Factory. *New Society*, 21, 513, 185-186.

Canadian Correctional Association (1965) Official Statement of Policy.

Carney, L.P. (1980) *Corrections : Treatment and Philosophy.* Englewood Cliffs : Prentice-Hall.

Carol, F.W., Smith & Hohn, R.H., (1979) Alienation in Prison Organisations—A Comparative Analysis. *Criminology*, 17, 2.

Carter, R.M., Glaser, D. & Wilkins, L.T. (Eds.) (1977) *Correctional Institutions.* New York : J.B. Lippin Colt.

Case, H.D., (1967) 'Doing time' in the Bucks County Prison. Doylestown. *Fed. Prab.*, 31, 3, 9-17.

Chapman, D., (1963) *Sociology and the Stereotype of the Criminal.* London : Tavistock.

Clemmer, D., (1958) *The Prison Community*. New York : Holt, Rinehart and Winston.

Cloward, R.A., (1960) Social Control in Prison. In Cloward, R.A. Ed., *Theoretical Status in the Social Organisation of the Prison*. New York : SSRC.

Cobean, S.C. and Power, P.W., (1978) The Role of the Family in the Rehabilitation of the Offender. *Inter. J. of Offender Therapy & Comparative Criminology*, 22, 1, 29.

Conso, G. (1973) In Prison : To Idle or to Work ? Arch. enale, 3, 1, 4, 60-63.

Datir, R.N., (1978) *Prison as a Social System*. Bombay : Popular Prakashan.

Deford, M.A., (1962) *Stone-Walls*. Philadelphia : Chilton.

Deimling, G., (1973) Educational and Vocational Training as Aids to Social Integration in Juvenile and Adult Corrections. *Recht Jugend Bildungsw*, 21, 1, 2, 23-29.

Desai, I.P., (1943) *Social Basis of Crime*. Unpublished Ph.D. Thesis, Bombay : University of Bombay.

Duffee, D., (1975) *Correctional Policy and Prison Organisation*. London : John Wiley & Sons.

Dumont, L., (1970) *Homo Hierarchious* : *The Caste System and Its Implications*. Delhi : Vikas.

Else, J. F. & Stephenson, K. D., (1974) Vicarious expiation : a theory of prison and social reform. *Crime and Delinquency*, 20, 4, 359-372.

Farmer, R., (1977) Cynicism : A Factor in Correctional Work. *J. Crim. Justice*, 5, 3, 237-246.

Ferguson, T., (1966) *Children in Care—and After*. London : Oxford U. Press.

Fleisher, B.M., (1966) The Effects of Income on Delinquency. *Amer. Eco. Rev.*, 56, 1, 118-137.

Fox, L. W. (1952) *The English Prison and Borstal System.* London : Routledge & Kegan Paul.

Fraze, J. (1950) *The Golden Bough.* New York : MacMillan.

Freeman, H.E. & Sherwood, C. C. (1970) *Social Research and Social Policy.* Englewood Cliffs : Prentice-Hall.

Freeman, H. E. & Showel, M., (1957) The Role of Family in Socialisation Process. J. of Social Psychology, 37, pp. 97-101.

Galway, E. J., (1948) *A Measurement of Effectiveness of a Reformatory Program.* Unpublished Ph.D. Dissertation., Ohio State Univ.

Gels, G. & Cavanagh, E., (1969) Recruitment and Retention of Correctional Personnel. *Crime and Delinquency.*, 12, 3, 227-239.

Glaser, D., (1964) The Effectiveness of a Prison and Parole System. Indianapolis : Bobbs-Merrill.

Glaser, D., (1971) Politicisation of Prisoners : A New Challenge to American Penology. *Amer. J. of Correct.*, 33, 6, 6-9.

Glaser, D., (1977) Concern with Theory in Correctional Evaluation Research. *Crime and Delinquency*, April, 173-179.

Gleason, S.E., (1978) Hustting : The Inside Economy of Prison. *Federal Probation*, 42, 2, 32-40.

Glueck, Sheldon & Glueck, Eleanor (1930) : *500 Criminal Careers.* New York : Knopf.

Goffman, D., (1961) *Asylums.* Garden City : Anchor.

Goldschmidt (1960) *Exploring the Ways of Mankind.* New York: Holf, Rinehart & Winston.

Goode, W., (1959) The Sociology of the Family. In Merton, R., et. al., *Sociology Today.* New York : Basic Books.

Gordon, A. B. (1971) Correctional Industries Committee. *Mil. Police J.*, 21, 2, 10-11.

Gordon, J.J., (1967) The Pennsylvania Public Offenders Program of the Pennsylvania Bureau of Vocational Rehabilitation. *Prison J.*, 47, 1, 39-42.

Govt. of India (1970) *Model Prison Manual.* Faridabad : GOI Press.

Grant. R. A. (1964) Public Offenders, Rehabilitative and Correctional Services. *Rehabi Research*, 5, 6, 1-4.

Grant, R.A., (1967) Vocational Rehabilitation and Correction. *J. Correct. Educ.*, 19, 1, 14-16 and 23-24.

Greenberg, D.F. & Stender, F. (1972) The Prison as a Lawless Agency. *Buffalo Law Rev.*, 21, 3, 799-838.

Grunhut, M., (1952) *Penal Reform.* New York : Oxford.

Grupp, S. & Verin, J., (1968) Work Release for Short-term Offenders in France and the United States. *Canad. J. Corrections*, 10, 3, 490-504.

Grutzner, W., (1971) Prison Guards Caught in the Conflict. *Z. Strafvollzug*, 20, 1, 8-14.

Guenther, A.L. & Guenther, M.Q., (1974) Screws Vs Thugs. *Society*, 11, 5, 42-50.

Halleck, S.L., (1967) *Psychiatry and the Dilemmas of Crime.* New York : Harper & Row.

Haney, C., Banks, C. & Zimbardo, P., (1973) Interpersonal Dynamics in a stimulated Prison. *Int. J. Criminol. Penol.*, 1, 1, 69-97.

Harding Le Riche, W. (1975) Are convicts human ? *Canad. Society Forens. Sci.*, 18, 1, 31-35.

Haynes, F. E., (1935) *Criminology.* New York : McGraw.

Heyns, G., (1964) What the Public Should Know about Adult Correction. *Federal Probation,* 28, 1.

Hibbert, C., (1963) *The Roots of Evil.* Penguin.

Hodgkin, N., (1972) The New Careers Project at Vacaville : a Californian Experiment. *Howard J, Penol. Crime Prev.*, 13, 3, 184-211.

Holder, T., (1978) A Review and Perspective of HRD Program in Corrections. *Crim. Justice Rev.*, 3, 2, 7-17.

Holt, Norman, (1977) Prison Management in the Next Decade. *The Prison Journal.*, 47, 2, 16-30.

Hooper, H.M., (1964) The Modernization of Canada's Jails. *Canad. J. Corrections*, 6, 4, 453-462.

Huffman, A.V., (1960) Sex Deviation in a Prison Community. *J. of Social Therapy*, 6, 179.

Hulin, C. L. & Maher, B. A., (1959) Changes in Attitudes towards Law Concomitant with Imprisonment. *J. of Criminal Law, Crimi. & Police Science*, 50, 3, 245-248.

Hutton, J.H., (1961) *Caste in India.* Oxford University Press, Bombay.

Hyman, J.M., (1977) Alienation and Prisonisation. *Bowling Gree OH Criminology*, 15, 2, 263-265.

Johnson, E.H., (1964) *Crime, Correction and Society.* Homewood : Dorsey.

——— (1970) Report on an Innovation—State work-release programmes. *Crime and Delinquency*, 16, 4, 417-426.

Johnson, S. F., (1967) A teacher's view of Vocational Training within a Penal Establishment. *Prison Serv. J.*, 7, 25, 26-30.

Jones, H., (1956) *Crime and the penal system.* London : University Tutorial Press.

Karve, I., (1953) *Kinship Organisation in India.* Poona : Deccan College.

Kellerhals, H., (1959) Integration of Prison Labour with National Economy. *Inter. Rev. Crim. Policy*, 14, 21-22.

Kellogg, V., (1950) Inside Women's Prison. Collier's, 125, 22.

Khan, M.Z., (1976) Work Programme in Correctional Institutions. *Social Defence*, 11, 43, 12-33.

——— (1981) Inmates of Jails. In Joshi and Bhatia : *Social Defence Research in India.* Allahabad : A. H. Wheeler.

Khan, M. Z., (1982) Crime. *In Encyclopaedia of Social Work* (forthcoming). New Delhi : Ministry of Social Welfare.

Khan, M. Z. and Chilad, B.S., (1982) Policy Shifts in Institutional Correction in India. *Indian J. of Social Work.*,

Khan, M. Z., & Unnithan, P., (1978) Capability of Inmates and their Interest in Work-Programmes at the Central Prison, Madras. *The Indian Journal of Social Work*, 39, 1, 9-26.

Kirkpatrick, A. M., (1974) The Prison Dilemma. *Canadian J. of Criminol. and Correction*, 16, 3, 282-290.

Koerber, L., (1934) *Soviet Russia Fights Crime*. Routledge & Kegan Paul.

Konopka, G., (1974) Corrections and Human Dignity. *Georgian J. Corrections*, 3, 1, 49-57.

Korn, R.R. & McCorkle, L.W., (1959) *Criminology and Penology*. New York : Holt, Rinehart & Winston.

Likert, R., (1961) *New Patterns of Management*. New York : McGraw Hill.

Lipton, D., Martinson, R. and Wilks., (1975) *The Effectiveness of Correctional Treatment*. New York : Praeger.

Lourdjane, A. (1972) Labour of Prisoners in French Prisons. *Rev. Penit. Droit. Penal.*, 96, 3, 549-556.

Mabli, J. et. al., (1979) Age and Prison Violence. *Crim. Justice Behav.*, 19, 6, 175-186.

Macht, M. W. & Seidl. F. W., (1977) Measuring Inmate Morale. *Soc. Work*, 22, 4, 284-289.

Maier, N.A., (1965) *Psychology in Industry*. New Delhi : Oxford & IBH.

Malinowski, B., (1926) : *Crime and Custom in a Savage Society*. New York : Humanities Press.

Mannheim, H., Ed. (1972) *Pioneers in Criminology*. Montelair : Patterson Smith.

Martinson, R., (1974) What Works ? Questions and Answers about Prison Reform. *The Public Interest*, 22.

McClean, J.D., (1964) Corrective Training : Decline and Fall. *Criminal Law Review*, Nov., 745-762.

McClintock, F.M., (1970) The Dark Figure in Council of Europe : *Collected Studies in Criminological Research.*

McCollum, S.G., (1973) New Designs for Correctional Education and Training Programmes. *Fed. Probation*, 37, 2, 6-11.

McCorkle, L. W., et. al., (1958) The Highfields Story : An Experimental Treatment Project for Youthful Offenders. New York : Henry Holt.

McGrath, W. T. (1965) Prison Pay and Discharge Provisions in Canada. *Canadian Correct.*, 8, 4, 13.

Miller, M. D., (1972) Vocational Training in Prisons : Some Social Policy Implication. *Federal Probation*, 36, 3, 19-21.

Mintern, L. & Lambert, W. W., (1964) *Mothers of Six Cultures.* New York : John Wiley.

Montagano, O., (1971) Programme Outlining Educational and Training Activities in Vocational Courses for the Scholastic Year 1971-72. *Rass. Studi Penitenz.*, 21, 6, 25-33.

Moran, M. R., (1954) *Inmate Concept of Self.* (Unpublished) Ph.D. Dissertation, Ohio S. University.

Morris, N. (1974) *The Future of Imprisonment.* Chicago:Chicago University Press.

Morris, N. & Hawkins, G., (1970) Rehabilitation : Rhetoric or Reality. *Federal Probation*, 34, pp. 12-13.

Murton, T.O., (1976) *The Dilemma of Prison Reform.* New York : Holt, Rinehart & Winston.

Nair, I. M., (1969) *The role of prison industries in the rehabilitation of discharged prisoners.* Unpublished Ph.D. Thesis, Agra : Agra University.

NCCD News (1964) *Work Release Program Establishment in Los Angles County.* 43, 5, 7. New York : NCCD.

Nelson, E. K., (1966) Strategies for Action in Meeting Correctional Manpower and Programme Needs. *Crime and Delinquency.*, 12, 3, 221-226.

Nie, N. H., et. al., (1970) *Statistical Package for Social Sciences.* New York ; McGraw Hill.

Nijboer, J. A., (1971) Training during Detention and Recidivism. *Ned. T. Criminol.*, 13, 4, 211-220.

Orland, L., (1975) *Prisons : Houses of Darkness.* New York : The Free Press.

Orsagh, T. & Witte, D., (1981) Economic Status and Crime : Implications for offender rehabilitation. *J. Cl. and Crim.*, 72, 3, 1055-1071.

Osborne, T. M., (1928) *Within Prison Walls.* New York : Doubleday & Appleton.

Page, J. D. (1947) *Abnormal Psychology.* New York : McGraw.

Park, R.E. & Burgess, E. W., (1924) *Introduction to the Science of Sociology.* Chicago : Chicago U. Press.

Peretti, P. O., (1969) Educational Rehabilitation : Prisoners' Attitude and Inmate Attendance. *Prison Serv. Journal*, 8, 30, 40-45.

——— (1970) Desocialisation—Resocialisation Process within Prison Walls. *Canadian J. of Correction*, 12, 59-66.

Peretti, P.O. & Hooker, M., (1976) Social Role Self Perception of State Prison Guards. *Crim. Justice Behav.*, 3, 2, 187-196.

Pillai, U. N., (1959) Problems of Prison Labour in Underdeveloped Countries. *Inter. Rev. of Crim. Policy*, 14, 3-9.

Pogrebin, M., (1974) Administrative Demands as Impediments to Treatment in Correctional Institutions in Allen, HE & Beran, N.J., (1974), *Reform in Correction.* New York : Praeger.

Ponti, G. & Sacchi, E., (1975) The Use of New Techniques of Management Instruction in the Training of Top Management of Penal Institutions. *Revss Stud Penitenz.*, 25, 5, 775-793.

Prabhu, P. N., (1954) *Hindu Social Organisation.* Bombay : Popular.

Radzinowicz, L. (1971) Economic Pressures. In Radzinowicz, L. and Wolfgang, M.E. : *The Criminal in Society.* New York : Basic Books.

Ranney, A. (1968) The Study of Policy Content. *Items*, 22, 25-31.

Reasons, C. E. & Kaplan, C. E., (1975) Ten Down the Wall ? Some Functions of Prisons. *Crime and Delinq.*, 21, 4, 360-372.

Reinhardt, J. M., (1968) Prison Education as on Aid to Therapy. *Int. J. Offenders Ther.*, 12, 3, 113-118.

Riscalla, L. M., (1975) Staff Relationships : Implications for Effective Service. *Correct. Soc. Psychiat. J. Behav. Technol. Methods Ther.* 21, 3, 20-22.

Roberts, A. R., (1969) Development Perspective of Correctional Education. *Amer. J. Correct.*, 31, 3, 14-17.

Robinson, J. & Smith, G., (1971) The Effectiveness of Correctional Programs. *Crime and Delinquency*, 67.

Saksena H.C. (1960) Extramural Employment of Prisoners in India. *Journal of Correctional Work*, 26-38.

Schmidt, F. K., (1971) The Jail as a Treatment Centre. *Police*, 16, 3, 19-22.

Sellin, T., (1967) Reflections on penal servitude. *Rev. Estud. Penit.*, 22, 174, 505-519.

Sepe, A. S. & De Trucco, A. M. I., (1973) New guidelines for the psychological education of prison personnel. *Quad. Criminol. Clin.*, 15, 4, 437-451.

Shalleck, J. & Berry, L. A., (1972) *Prison.* New York : Grossman Publishers.

Shrivastava, R. S., (1971) *Jodhpur Central Jail : A Sociological Study of an Indian Prison.* Unpublished Ph.D. Thesis. Jodhpur : University of Jodhpur.

Singer, N.M. (1973) Incentives and the use of Prison Labour. *Crime and Delinquency*, 19, 2, 200-211.

Singer, N. M., (1977) Economic Implications of standards for Correctional Institutions. *Crime and Delinquency*, Jan., Issue.

Singh, I. J., (1979) *Indian Prison.* Delhi : Concept Publishing Co.,

Singh, U. P., (1973) *Personality of Criminals.* Agra : Sri Ram & Co.,

Sjoquist, S., (1973) Property Crime and Economic Behaviour : Some Empirical Results. *Am. Eco. Rev.*, 63, 439.

Soine, V., (1964) "Finland's Open Institutions". *Federal Probation*, XXVIII, 9, 19-20.

Srinivas, M. N., (1966) *Social Change in Modern India.* Los Angeles : California U. Press.

Srivastava, S. P., (1977) *The Indian Prison Community.* Lucknow : Pustak Kendra.

Sutherland, E. H. and Cressey, D. R., (1968) *Principles of Criminology.* Bombay : Times of India Press.

Switzer, M. E., (1967) Vocational Rehabilitation and Correction. *Fed. Probation*, 21, 3, 12-17.

Sykes, G. M., (1958) *The Society of Captives.* Princeton : Princeton University Press.

———— (1978) *Criminology.* New York : Harcourt Brace Jovanovich.

Tabasz, T. F., (1975) *Towards an Economics of Prisons.* Westmead : Lexington Books.

Taft, D. R., (1956) *Criminology.* New York : MacMillan.

Talbert, J., (1973) Prison Mate under Direct Management. *Rev. Peivitent, Droit Penal.*, 97, 1, 9-22.

Tannebaum, F., (1957) *Crime and the Community.* New York : Columbia University Press.

Tappan, P. W., (1960) *Crime, Justice and Correction.* New York: McGraw-Hill.

Task Force Report : Correction (1967) Washington : GPO.

Taylor, E. (1930) *Anthropology.* London : Watts & Co.,

Thomas, C. W., (1977) Theoretical Perspectives on Prisonisation. *J. of Crim. Law & Criminol*; 68, 1, 135-145.

Trivedi, B. V., (1977) Work Incentives in Indian Correctional Institutions. *J. of Correctional Work*, 32.

——— (1978) Relevance of Work-programmes in Institutional Correction in India. *Indian Journal of Criminology*, 6, 2.

——— (1981) Opinion of Jail Officials about inmates. *Indian Journal of Criminology*, 9, 2.

——— (1980) Attitude of Inmates towards Jail Officials. *Social Defence*, 15, 60.

——— (1984) Work Programmes for Jail Inmates in Model Prison, *Indian J. of Criminology*, Vol. 12, No. 1, pp. 8-14.

United Nations (1955) *Proceedings of the First United Nations Congress on the Prevention of Crime and Treatment of Offenders.* New York : United Nations.

Unnithan, N. P. & Khan, M. Z. (1978) Incentive Pattern in Work Programmes at the Central Prison, Madras. *Ind. J. of Social Work*, 39, 2, 175-185.

Unnithan, N. P. & Khan, M. Z., (1979) The Acquisition of Skills by Inmates in Work Programmes at the Central Prison, Madras. *Ind. J. of Social Work*, 40, 1, 1-14.

Unnithan, N. P. & Trivedi, B. V., (1978) The Job-competence of the Vocational Staff in two Indian Prisons. *Social Defence*, 14, 54.

Uttar Pradesh Jail Industries Inquiry Committee (1955) Report., Lucknow.

Vanbuskirk, D. E., (1964) Correctional Education through Electronic Data Processing. *Amer. J. Correction.*, 26, 1, 16-18.

Van der Werff (1981) Recidivism and Special Deterrence. *British J. of Criminology*, 21, 2, 136-147.

Verin, J., (1964) Work Release in France. *Min. of Justice, Vendome Prison*, 44, 1, 28-34.

——— (1973) The Prison Guard. *Rev. Sci. Crim. Droit. Pen. Coup.*, 4, 940-946.

Vidya Bhushan (1970) Prison Administration in India. New Delhi : S. Chand.

Wellford, C. F., (1973) Contact and Commitment in a Correctional Community. *British J. of Criminology*, 13, 2, 108-20.

Wenk, E. A. & Frank, C., (1973) Some Progress in the Evaluation of Institutional Programmes. *Fed. Prob.*, 37, 3, 30-37.

Whiting, B. B., (1963) *Six Cultures*. New York : John Wiley.

Witte, D., and Reid, W. H., (1980) An exploration of the determinants of labour market performance for prison releases. *Journal of Urban Economics*, 8, 313.

Wilkins, L. T. (1969) *Evaluation of Penal Measures*, New York : Random House.

Wofe, J., et. al., (1978) Vocational Training Facilities in Adult Correction. *Oldenburg Criminal J.*, 10, 11-20.

Wright, M., (1972) Prison Industry. *New Society*, 22, 528, 402.

Zeeman, E. C. et. al., (1977) A Model for Prison Disturbances. *British J. of Crim.*, 17, 3, 251-263.

Zeigler, H., (1974) Prison : What's It All About ? *Society* ; 11, 5, 67-69.

Zielinska, E. (1976) A New Type of Sanction in Poland : The Non-custodial Curtailment of Liberty. *Int. J. Offend. Ther. Cimpar. Criminal.*, 20, 1, 65-70.

Index

OUR OUTSTANDING PUBLICATIONS

Ahangar, Mohd. Altaf Hussain	Customary Succession Among Muslims.	1986	175.00
Amir Hussain, IAS	A Trinbe in Turmoil : Socio-Economic Study of Jammu Gujars of Uttar Pradesh.	1986	150.00
Balasubamanian, M.	Nehru : A Study in Secularism.	1980	45.00
Banerjea, Pramathanath	Public Administration in Ancient India.	1985	125.00
Barman, Kiran	Public Debt Management in India.	1986	150.00
Baruah, A.K.	Systems Analysis in Political Science : A Marxit Critique of David Easton.	1987	125.00
Bawa, Noorjahan	People's Participation Development Adm. in India.	1985	125.00
Bayti, Jamnalal	Readings in Education.	1986	150.00
Bayti, Jamnalal	Studies in the problems of Education in the third world.	1987	150.00
Bhattacharjee, Debasish	Bureacracy and Development in Meghalaya.	1986	150.00
Bhattacharya, Mohit	Management of Urban Government in India	1976	50.00
Bhattacharya, Mohit	Bureaucracy and development Administration.	1979	50.00
Bhargava, P.K.	Essays on Indian Economic Planning.	1985	90.00
Bhargava, P.K.	Some Aspects of Indian Public Finances.	1984	125.00
Bijan Mohanta	Administrative Development of Arunachal Pradesh, 1875-1975.	1984	150.00
Biswas, Atreyi	Political, Social and Cultural History of Ancient India (H).	1982	125.00
Centre for Policy Research, N. Delhi	Population, Poverty and Hope.	1983	300.00
Chaudhari, R.L.	The Concept of Secularism in Indian Constitution	1987	200.00
Desmukh, C.D.	Amarakosa : Gems from the Treasure House of Sanskrit Words.	1981	90.00

Dey, Bata K.	Bureaucracy Development and Public Management in India.	1978	80.00
Durrany, K S.	Religion in Society.	1983	200.00
Gabriel, Soloman	Foreign policy of Canada	1987	125.00
Ghosh, Partha S.	Sino-Soviet Relations : U.S. Perception and Policy Resp.	1981	100.00
Ghosh, Shubhra	Female Criminals in India.	1986	125.00
Handa, K.L.	Programme Performance Budgeting.	1979	75.00
Jagannadham, V.	Administration and Social Change.	1978	60.00
Jain, Anil Kumar	Some Aspects of Income-Tax Administration in India.	1983	100.00
Jain, D.K.	Project Planning and Appraisal in Planned Economy : The Indian Context.	1981	75.00
Jain, R.B. and P.N. Chaudhuri	Bureaucratic Values in Development.	1982	120.00
Jain, R.B.	Comparative Legislative Behaviour.	1980	50.00
Kaushik, S.N.	Pakistan under Bhutto's Leadership.	1985	175.00
Kamble, N.D.	Bonded Labour in India.	1982	60.00
Kamble, N.D.	Migrants in Indian Metropolis.	1982	75.00
Kedia, Kusum Lata	Local Finance in an Indian State : Municipal Finance of Varanasi Division Since 1951-	1986	200.00
Khan, Mumtaz Ali	Scheduled Caste and their Status in India.	1980	75.00
Khan, Mumtaz Ali	Status of Rural Women in India.	1982	75.00
Khan, Mumtaz Ali	Social Legislation and the Rural Poor.	1981	50.00
Khan, Mumtaz Ali	Muslims in the Process of Rural Development in India	1984	150.00
Mandal, B.B.	Tribais at the Polls : A Study of Khunti in Chotanagpur.	1986	90.00
Madan, J.C.	Indian Police.	1980	110.00

Mahendra Singh	Indo-U.S. Relations : A Political Study.	1985	75.00
Malik, Inder Lal	Dalai Lamas of Tibet.	1984	90.00
Menon, M. Indu	Status of Muslim Women in India.	1981	50.00
Mishra, Upendra	Caste and Politics in India.	1986	225.00
Mishra, S.N. and Kushal Sharma	Problems and Prospects of Rural Development in India.	1983	80.00
Mohan, N. Shantha	Status of Nurses in India.	1985	60.00
Mukarji, Nirmal and Ashis Banerjee	Democracy Federalism and the future of Indias Unity	1987	60.00
Pal, J.J.	Jinnah and the creation of Pakistan.	1985	75.00
Paliwal, M.R.	Social Change and Education.	1984	175.00
Paliwal, M.R.	The Teacher Education on the Move : Today and Tomorrow.	1985	225.00
Paliwal, M.R.	Differential Effectiveness of Micro-learning.	1984	50.00
Pai Panandiker, V.A. and Arun Sud.	Changing Political Representation in India.	1983	65.00
Pai Panandikar, V.A. and Ajay K. Mehra	People's Participation in Family Planning.	1987	160.00
Pai Panandiker, V.A., R.N. Bisnnoi and O.P. Sharma	Organisational Policy for Family Planning.	1983	125.00
Pai Panandiker, V.A. and P.N. Chaudhuri	Demographic Transition in Goa and its Policy Implications.	1983	40.00
Panda, Basudev	Indian Bureaucracy : An Inside Story.	1978	60.00
Pandey, K.K.	Rural Development in India : Continuity and Change.	1986	125.00
Pandey, Jawaharlal	State Politics in India.	1982	90.00
Partap Singh	Urban Government in India.	1978	45.00
Pillai, G. Narayana	Social Background of Political Leadership in India.	1983	90.00
Rai, Haridwar and S.P. Singh	Current Ideas and Issues in Indian Administration.	1979	70.00

Rajgopal, P.R.	Communal Violence in India.	1987	140.00
Rajjan Lal and Kidwai, Nasira	Practical Cataloguing Procedure (Hindi).	1980	95.00
Rastogi, P.N.	India 1981-86 : A forecaste on Economic, Political and Social Developments.	1982	50.00
Reddy, P. Ranjani	The Role of Dominant Caste in Indian Politics.	1987	150.00
Rawlinson, H.G.	Shivaji the Maratha : his Life and Time.	1984	75.00
Ray, B. Datta	The Emergence and Role of Middle Class in North East India.	1983	100.00
Ray, B. Datta	The Pattern and Problems of Population in North-East India.	1986	250.00
Rita Khanna	Agricultural Mechanisation and Social Change in India.	1983	125.00
Roy, R.C., IAS	State Public Enterprise in India.	1986	200.00
Saksena, H.S.	Safeguards for Scheduled Castes and Tribes : Founding Father's View.	1981	200.00
Seshadri, K.	Studies in the problems of the third world.	1986	175.00
Seshadri, K.	Studies in Indian Polity.	1986	150.00
Sharma, P.D.	Police and Criminal Justice Administration in India.	1985	125.00
Sharma, P.D.	Police, Polity and People in India.	1981	125.00
Sharma, R.N. & Bakshi Santosh	Tribes and Tribal Development : Select Bibliography.	1984	250.00
Sharma, T.R.	New Challenges in Indian Politics.	1986	175.00
Shrivastava, M.P.	Problems of Accountability of Public Enterprises in India.	1986	225.00
Sikka, R.P.	The Civil Service in India.	1984	150.00
Sinha, R.P.	Social Dimensions of Trade Unionism in India.	1986	90.00
Singh, L.P.	Electoral Reform.	1986	95.00
Singh, L.P.	India's Foreign Policy.	1980	55.00
Singh, S.P.	Perspectives in Indian Politics and Administration.	1981	60.00

Singh, S.S.	Administration of Natural Justice in India.	1986	250.00
Singh, S.S. and S. Sundram	Emerging Harijan Elite : A Study of their Identity.	1987	125.00
Sundeep Khanna, IAS	Civil Administration in India.	1983	60.00
Trivedi, B.V.	Prison Administration in India : Model Prison Programme.	1987	175.00
Verma, S.P.	Indian Parliamentarians : A Study of the Socio-Political Background.	1986	90.00
Vijay Kumar	India and Srilanka-China Relations 1948-84.	1986	125.00
Wishwakarama, R.K.	Urban and Regional Planning Policy in India.	1981	75.00